A Zen Story A Day

A Zen Story A Day

Rahul Karn

CONTENTS

CONTENTS

CONTENTS

CONTENTS

CONTENTS

CONTENTS

CONTENTS

CONTENTS

CONTENTS

CONTENTS

CONTENTS

CONTENTS

CONTENTS

CONTENTS

CONTENTS

CONTENTS

CONTENTS

CONTENTS

A
ZEN
STORY
A
DAY

A COLLECTION OF 365 ZEN STORIES

Rahul Karn

Dedicated To

The Buddha

PREFACE

Dear Zen Friends,

There is an ancient saying that an apple a day keeps the doctor away. It ticked me with an idea about trying the same with Zen Stories. Apple is for physical health and Zen is there for mental health. In the modern age, with the advent of smart mobiles, people's lifestyle has dramatically changed. Many of the people, the moment they wake up, check their mobile phones. Of course, internet provide you with lot of useful information; but at the same time, it might also dump all kind of nonsense rubbish into your mind, making your brain a rubbish bin! So, to make a zensational start of the day, I initiated a Facebook page called Zensational Stories which was a great success. Some people check the newspaper early in the morning, which again does the same thing as the internet does. So, I also decided to come up with a book which can give you some positive thoughts early in the morning. And here you have: "A Zen Story A Day...".

Imagine starting your day with a Zen Story. It will keep you charged with a positivity throughout your day. These Zen Stories have different messages. Some motivate you to find the truth yourself, others motivate you to meditate. Some are there to tickle you whereas some are there to provoke a thought in you. Sometimes a single story has multiple messages. That's why they are timeless.

These Zen Stories are taken from various timeless classics. Some of the stories have come in multiple classics and therefore I have not mentioned the source of each and every story, unless it is very rare. Rather I have provided a detailed bibliography from where these stories have been compiled.

One more thing, while it's good to have an apple a day, it's not good for your health to eat all 365 apples in a single day. Similarly, these stories are also there to be enjoyed slowly. Don't take it as a novel and finish it in one go. It will defeat the purpose of these stories.

I am sure these stories will be the starting point to take you on a more serious journey of Zen.

Should you have any queries, please don't hesitate to contact me on zensationalstories@gmail.com.

Have a Zensational time ahead!

Your Zen Friend,
Rahul Karn
Melbourne
8th of Feb 2020

1

Hard Work

Once, Zen Master Kwon began meditating from morning to night. As soon as the sun would set, he would beat his fists against the ground in frustration and cry out, "I have lost another day without realizing my Mind." He continued this way every day until he was fully awakened.

~ The Great Matter of Life and Death ~
~ Zen Master Kyong Ho ~

Bodhidharma Pacifies the Mind

Shenkuang [Huike] went over to the Shaolin temple and day and night beseeched Bodhidharma for instruction. The Master always sat in zazen facing the wall and paid no attention to his entreaties. One evening in December, there was a snowstorm but Shenkuang stood unmoving before Bodhidharma right through the night. In the morning, the snow reached above his knees. Bodhidharma took pity on him and said, "You have been standing in the snow for a long time. What is it you're seeking?" Shenkuang said in bitter tears, "I beseech you, Master, open the gate of the Dharma and save all of us beings." Bodhidharma said, "The incomparable truth of the Buddhas can only be attained by constant striving—practicing what cannot be practiced, bearing the unbearable. How can you, with your small virtue and wisdom, and your easygoing and conceited mind, dare to aspire to the true teaching? It is only so much labour lost." With this, Shenkuang secretly drew his knife and cut off his arm, placing it before Bodhidharma. At this, Bodhidharma relented and accepted him as a disciple, giving him the Dharma name Huike (Light of

Wisdom). Huike said, "Your disciple's mind has no peace yet. I beg you, Master, please put it to rest." Bodhidharma said, "Bring me your mind, and I will put it to rest." Huike said, "I have searched for my mind, but I cannot find it." Bodhidharma said, "I have completely put it to rest for you." **"YES!", said Hui K'o, and laughed.**

3

The Tunnel

Zenkai, the son of a samurai, journeyed to Edo and there became the retainer of a high official. He fell in love with the official's wife and was discovered. In self-defense, he slew the official. Then he ran away with the wife.

Both of them later became thieves. But the woman was so greedy that Zenkai grew disgusted. Finally, leaving her, he journeyed far away to the province of Buzen, where he became a wandering mendicant.

To atone for his past, Zenkai resolved to accomplish some good deed in his lifetime. Knowing of a dangerous road over a cliff that had caused death and injury to many persons, he resolved to cut a tunnel through the mountain there.

Begging food in the daytime, Zenkai worked at night digging his tunnel. When thirty years had gone by, the tunnel was 2,280 feet long, 20 feet high and 30 feet wide.

Two years before the work was completed, the son of the official he had slain, who was a skillful swordsman, found Zenkai out and came to kill him in revenge.

"I will give you my life willingly," said Zenkai. "Only let me finish this work. On the day it is completed, then you may kill me."

So the son awaited the day. Several months passed and Zenkai kept digging. The son grew tired of doing nothing and began to help with the digging. After he had helped for more than a year, he came to admire Zenkai's strong will and character.

At last the tunnel was completed and the people could use it and travel safely.

"Now cut off my head," said Zenkai. "My work is done."

"How can I cut off my own teacher's head?" asked the younger man with tears in his eyes.

A bond of love forged in the fire of hate.

4

The Last Will and Testament

Ikkyu, a famous Zen teacher of the Ashikaga era, was the son of the emperor. When he was very young, his mother left the palace and went to study Zen in a temple. In this way Prince Ikkyu also became a student. When this mother passed on, she left him a letter. It read:

To Ikkyu:

I have finished my work in this life and am now returning into Eternity. I wish you to become a good student and to realize your Buddha-nature. You will know if I am in hell and whether I am always with you or not.

If you become a man who realizes that the Buddha and his follower Bodhidharma are your own servants, you may leave off studying and work for humanity. The Buddha preached for forty-nine years and in all that time found it not necessary to speak one word. You ought to know why. But if you don't and yet wish to, avoid thinking fruitlessly.

Your Mother,

Not born, not dead.

September first.

P.S. The teaching of Buddha was mainly for the purpose of enlightening others. If you are dependent on any of its methods, you are naught but an ignorant insect. There are 80,000 books on Buddhism and if you should read all of them and still not see your own nature, you will not understand even this letter. This is my will and testament.

5

It Will Pass

A student went to his meditation teacher and said, "My meditation is horrible! I feel so distracted, or my legs ache, or I'm constantly falling asleep. It's just horrible!"

"It will pass," the teacher said matter-of-factly.

A week later, the student came back to his teacher. "My meditation is wonderful! I feel so aware, so peaceful, so alive! It's just wonderful!'

"It will pass," the teacher replied matter-of-factly.

6

Nothing Exists

Yamaoka Tesshu, as a young student of Zen, visited one master after another. He called upon Dokuon of Shokoku.

Desiring to show his attainment, he said: "The mind, Buddha, and sentient beings, after all, do not exist. The true nature of phenomena is emptiness. There is no realization, no delusion, no sage, no mediocrity. There is no giving and nothing to be received."

Dokuon, who was smoking quietly, said nothing. Suddenly he whacked Yamaoka with his bamboo pipe. This made the youth quite angry.

"If nothing exists," inquired Dokuon, "where did this anger come from?"

Present Moment

A Japanese warrior was captured by his enemies and thrown into prison. That night he was unable to sleep because he feared that the next day he would be interrogated, tortured, and executed. Then the words of his Zen master came to him, "Tomorrow is not real. It is an illusion. The only reality is now." Heeding these words, the warrior became peaceful and fell asleep.

8

Laughter

Buddha was to give a special talk one day, and thousands of followers had come from miles around.

When Buddha appeared, he was holding a flower. Time passed, but Buddha said nothing. He just looked at the flower. The crowd grew restless, but Mahakashyapa, who could restrain himself no longer, laughed.

Buddha beckoned him over, handed him the flower, and said to the crowd, "I have the eye of the true teaching. All that can be given with words I have given to you; but with this flower, I give to Mahakashyapa the key to this teaching."

~ Osho: A Bird On The Wing ~

The World-Honored One Ascends the Teaching Seat

One day the World-Honored One ascended the teaching seat and the assembly came together.

Mahākāśyapa struck the mallet and announced: "The World-Honored One has just expounded the dharma."

The World-Honored One descended from the teaching seat.

10

The Game of Chess

A young man who had a bitter disappointment in life went to a remote monastery and said to the abbot: 'I am disillusioned with life and wish to attain enlightenment to be freed from these sufferings. But I have no capacity for sticking long at anything. I could never do long years of meditation and study and austerity; I should relapse and be drawn back to the world again, painful though I know it to be. Is there any short way for people like me?' 'There is,' said the abbot, 'if you are really determined. Tell me, what have you studied, what have you concentrated on most in your life?' 'Why, nothing really. We were rich, and I did not have to work. I suppose the thing I was really interested in was chess. I spent most of my time at that.'

The abbot thought for a moment, and then said to his attendant: 'Call such-and-such a monk, and tell him to bring a chessboard and men.' The monk came with the board and the abbot set up the men. He sent for a sword and showed it to the two. 'O monk,' he said, 'you have vowed obedience to me as your abbot, and now I require it of you. You will play a game of chess with this youth, and if you lose I shall cut off your head with this sword. But I promise that you will be re-born in paradise. If you win, I shall cut off the head of this man; chess is the only thing he has ever tried hard at, and if he loses, he deserves to lose his head also.' They looked at the abbot's face and saw that he meant it: he would cut off the head of the loser.

They began to play. With the opening moves the youth felt the sweat trickling down to his heels as he played for his life. The chessboard became the whole world; he was entirely concentrated on it. At first, he had somewhat the worst of it, but then the other made an inferior move and he seized his chance to launch a strong attack. As his opponent's position crumbled, he looked covertly at him. He saw a face of intelligence and sincerity, worn with years of austerity and effort. He thought of his own worthless life, and a wave of compassion came over him. He deliberately made a blunder and then another blunder, ruining his position and leaving himself defenceless.

The abbot suddenly leant forward and upset the board.

The two contestants sat stupefied. 'There is no winner and no loser,' said the abbot slowly, 'there is no head to fall here.

Only two things are required,' and he turned to the young man, 'complete concentration, and compassion. You have to-day learnt them both. You were completely concentrated on the game, but then in that concentration you could feel compassion and sacrifice your life for it. Now stay here a few months and pursue our training in this spirit and your enlightenment is sure.' He did so and got it.

~ Zen and the Ways ~
~ Trevor Leggett ~

Master's Compassion

It happened once, a Zen Master was celebrating his master's birthday. The master had died. Somebody asked him, why are you celebrating? – Because as far as I know, the master denied you. He never accepted you as his disciple. You tried long, that I know. You tried again and again, that I know, but every time you were refused. You were never initiated by him. So why are you celebrating his birthday? Traditionally it is to be celebrated only by the accepted disciples.'

The master laughed and he said, 'precisely because he refused me, I celebrate. Now I can understand his compassion. If he had accepted me, I may have become just an imitator. Because he threw me into myself continuously, by and by I stood on my own feet. By and by I dropped the desperate search to cling to somebody else. He helped me. He was my master. In his rejection he accepted me.'

~ Nirvana: The Last Nightmare ~
~ Osho ~

12

Yunyan Tansheng

Yunyan Tansheng once told this parable: "Three travelers noticed a man standing on a small hill looking out over the landscape. The first traveler said, 'Look at that man. I suppose he's searching the country round for an animal that has wandered from his herd.'

"'Not at all,' the second said, 'he's simply watching out for a friend who's coming to visit him.'

"'Nonsense,' said the third. 'He's just enjoying the refreshing breeze.'

"The travelers argued among themselves but weren't able to come to agreement about why the man was standing there. When they came nearer to him, the first traveler called out to the man, 'Are you looking for a goat or sheep which has wandered from your flock?'

"'I don't have any flocks,' the man replied.

"'Then are you waiting for a friend?' the second asked.

"'No. I'm not waiting for a friend.'

"'Ah,' said the third. 'It must be as I expected that you're just enjoying the refreshing breeze.'

"'Not particularly,' the man said.

"'Then what are you doing?' the three travelers demanded.
"'I'm just standing here.'"

~ Zen Masters of China ~

The Short Staff

Shuzan held out his short staff and said, "If you call this a short staff, you oppose its reality. If you do not call it a short staff, you ignore the fact. Now what do you wish to call this?"

Returning to the Ordinary World

A monk asked Kegon, "How does an enlightened one return to the ordinary world?"

Kegon replied, "A broken mirror never reflects again; fallen flowers never go back to the old branches."

Any question?

One day Te-shan gave a sermon, in which he said, "When you question, you commit a fault. When you do not, you give offense."

A monk came forward and began to bow, whereupon the master struck him.

"I have just begun my bowing!" said the monk. "Why did you strike me?"

"If I wait for you to open your mouth, all will be over."

Tao

A monk asked Wei-kuan: "What is Tao?"

Wei-kuan replied: "What a fine mountain!"

"I am asking you about the Tao -- why do you talk up the mountain?"

"As long as you only know about the mountain," said Wei-kuan, "you can never attain the Tao."

The Most Eloquent Lecture

Butei, the emperor of Ryo, sent for Fu-Daishi to explain the Diamond Sutra (A scripture). On the appointed day Fu-Daishi came to the palace, mounted the platform, rapped on the table before him, then descended and, still not speaking, left!

Butei sat motionless for some minutes, whereupon Shiko, who had seen all that had happened, went up to him and said, "May I be so bold, Sir, as to ask whether you understood?"

The emperor shook his head sadly.

"What a pity," said Shiko, "Fu-Daishi has never been more eloquent!"

~ Osho: A Sudden Clash Of Thunder ~

A Mother's Advice

Jiun, a Shogun master, was a well-known Sanskrit scholar of the Tokugawa era. When he was young, he used to deliver lectures to his brother students.

His mother heard about this and wrote him a letter:

"Son, I do not think you became a devotee of the Buddha because you desired to turn into a walking dictionary for others. There is no end to information and commentation, glory and honor. I wish you would stop this lecture business. Shut yourself up in a little temple in a remote part of the mountain. Devote your time to meditation and in this way attain true realization."

Midnight Excursion

Many pupils were studying meditation under the Zen master Sengai. One of them used to arise at night, climb over the temple wall, and go to town on a pleasure jaunt. Sengai, inspecting the dormitory quarters, found this pupil missing one night and also discovered the high stool he had used to scale the wall. Sengai removed the stool and stood there in its place. When the wanderer returned, not knowing that Sengai was the stool, he put his feet on the master's head and jumped down into the grounds. Discovering what he had done, he was aghast.

Sengai said: "It is very chilly in the early morning. Do be careful not to catch cold yourself."

The pupil never went out at night again.

~ The Monk with Sweaty Palms ~

Kasan, a Zen teacher and monk, was to officiate at a funeral of a famous nobleman. As he stood there waiting for the governor of the province and other lords and ladies to arrive, he noticed that the palms of his hands were sweaty.

The next day he called his disciples together and confessed he was not yet ready to be a true teacher. He explained to them that he still lacked the sameness of bearing before all human beings, whether beggar or king. He was still unable to look through social roles and conceptual identities and see the sameness of being in every human. He then left and became the pupil of another master. He returned to his former disciples eight years later, enlightened.

~ A New Earth ~
~ Eckhart Tolle ~

Do Not Become Slaves to Any Holy Book

There was once a man who formed a religious cult and people regarded him as a very learned person. He had a few followers who recorded his instructions in a book. Over the years the book became voluminous with all sorts of instructions recorded therein. The followers were advised not to do anything without first consulting the holy book. Whenever the followers went and whatever they did, they would consult the book which served as the manual in guiding their lives. One day when the leader was crossing a timber bridge, he fell into the river. The followers were with him but none of them knew what to do under the circumstances. So they consulted the holy book.

"Help! Help!" the Master shouted, "I can't swim."

"Please wait a while Master. Please don't get drowned," they pleaded. "We are still searching in our holy book. There must be an instruction on what to do if you fell off from a wooden bridge into a river."

While they were thus turning over the pages of the holy

book in order to find out the appropriate instruction, the teacher disappeared in the water and drowned.

~ How to Live without Fear & Worry by Ven. K. Sri Dhammananda ~

Help

One day Chao-chou fell down in the snow, and called out, "Help me up!" A monk came and lay down beside him. Chao-chou got up and went away.

A Formal Discourse

One day Zen Master Yang-Chi (992-1049) got up to address a group seeking enlightenment and had only this to say:

"Ha! Ha! Ha! What's all this? Go to the back of the hall and have some tea!"

He then got down and departed!!!

Dream

When Zen master Takkan (1573-1645) was dying, his disciples asked him to write a death verse. He demurred at first, saying, "I have no last words." They pleaded with him, so he took up a brush, wrote the character for "dream," and passed away.

~ The Zen of Living and Dying ~
~ Philip Kapleau ~

The Enlightened

Once there was a well-known philosopher and scholar who devoted himself to the study of Zen for many years. On the day that he finally attained enlightenment, he took all of his books out into the yard and burned them all.

The First Thing

A novice said to a master, "I want to be a great man. What is the first thing I should do?"

The master answered, "Forget about being a great man."

Who Is He?

Zen Master Hoen said, "The past and future Buddhas, both are his servants. Who is he?"

A Smile in His Lifetime

Mokugen was never known to smile until his last day on earth. When his time came, he called his students and said, "You have studied with me for more than ten years. Show me your real interpretation of Zen. Whomever expresses this most clearly shall be my successor and receive my robe and bowl." Everyone watched Mokugen's severe face, but no one answered. Encho, a disciple of long standing, moved near the bedside and pushed Mokugen's medicine cup forward a few inches toward the bed. The teacher's face became even more severe. "Is that all you understand?" he demanded. Encho moved the cup back to its original place on the bedside table. A beautiful smile appeared on Mokugen's face. "You rascal," he said to Encho, "You have worked with me for ten years and have not yet seen my whole body. Take the robe and bowl. They belong to you."

[Note : Encho moved the medicine
cup toward his teacher.
Facing his teachers last
hours, he could not discuss
the interpretation of Zen. He

simply wanted his teacher to stay and live. "Is that all you understand?" the teacher asked. So Encho took back the cup: "If you insist, I will take back the medicine. Even though you pass away, please don't worry. I will take care of the temple." Mokugen smiled, for there was an assured feeling about his successor.]

Devil Teachings

Zen Master Isan said to Kyozan, "The Nirvana Sutra has about forty chapters of the Buddha's teaching; how many of these are devil teachings?"

Kyozan said, "All of them."

~ Kyozan, A True Man of Zen ~
~ Osho ~

The True Homage

Zen Master Rinzai arrived at Bodhidharma's memorial tower. The master of the tower said to him, "Venerable sir, will you pay homage first to the Buddha or to Bodhidharma?" "I don't pay homage to either the Buddha or to Bodhidharma," said Rinzai.
"Venerable sir, why are the Buddha and Bodhidharma your enemies?" asked the master of the tower.
Rinzai swung his sleeves and left.

The Ultimate Word

A monk asked, "What is 'the ultimate word'?"
Zen Master Jōshū coughed.
The monk said, "That's it, isn't it?"
Jōshū said, "Alas, they won't even let me cough."

~ Case 235 of Radical Zen ~

Bodhidharma and Emperor Wu

In 527 during the Liang Dynasty, Bodhidhama, the first Patriarch of Zen, visited the Emperor Wu of China.

Emperor Wu : 'How much merits have I earned for ordaining monks, building monasteries, having sutras copied and commissioning Buddha images?"

Bodhidharma : "None!"

Emperor Wu : "So what is the highest meaning of the holy truth?"

Bodhidharma : "There is no Holy Truth, there is only void."

Emperor Wu : 'Then who are you standing in front of me?"

Bodhidharma : "I don't know."

The emperor did not match him.

Finally, Bodhidharma crossed the Yangtze River and came to the Shaolin Temple. There he sat for nine years, facing the wall.

Later the emperor asked Shikô about it. Shikô said, "Does your Majesty know who that man is?" The emperor said, "I don't know." Shikô said, "He is the Mahasattva Avalokitesvara transmitting the Seal of the Buddha's mind." The emperor regretted what had happened and wanted to send an emissary to invite Bodhidharma back. Shikô said, "Your Majesty, don't try to send an emissary to fetch him back. Even if all the people in the land were to go after him, he would not return."

Later on, when Bodhidharma died:

Emperor Wu mourned Bodhidharma's death and personally wrote an inscription for his monument. It read, "Alas! I saw him without seeing him, I met him without meeting him, I encountered him without encountering him; now as before I regret this deeply." He further eulogized him by saying, "If your mind exists, you are stuck in the mundane for eternity; if your mind does not exist, you experience wondrous enlightenment instantly."

The Way

A monk asked Zen Master Tiantong Zongjue, "What is the Way?"

Tiantong said, "Stop making signposts at the crossroads."

34 |

The True Body

An inquirer asked Yanguan Qian, "Who was the Buddha?"

Yanguan replied by requesting of his visitor, "Would you please pass me that water-pitcher."

The inquirer looked around, saw the pitcher, and passed it to the master. Yanguan poured himself a cup of water and then asked the visitor to replace the pitcher. The visitor did so, then, thinking that perhaps Yanguan had not heard his original question, put it again: "About the Buddha—who was he?"

"Oh, yes," Yanguan said. "Well, you know, he's been dead a long time now."

~ Zen Masters of China ~

Danxia Burns a Buddha Image

Once when Zen master Danxia Tianran was staying at the temple Huilin si in the capital on a very cold day he took a wooden buddha image from the buddha hall, set it on fire, and warmed himself by the flames.

The temple supervisor happened to see this and scolded Danxia, saying, "How can you burn my wooden buddha!"

Danxia stirred the ashes with his staff and said, "I'm burning it to get the holy relics."[1]

The supervisor replied, "How could there be relics in a wooden buddha?"

"If there are no relics," Danxia answered, "then please give me the two attendant images to burn."

~ Case 44 of Entangling Vines ~

Sign of a Great Man

A monk asked Dasui, "What is the sign of a great man?" Dasui said, "He doesn't have a placard on his stomach."

The Great Communication

Zen Master Zhaozhou came to visit the monastery of Zen Master Baoshou. In the meditation hall Baoshou sat down facing away from him. Zhaozhou spread out his sitting cushion and bowed. Baoshou got up and went into the abbot's quarters. Zhaozhou picked up his meditation cushion and went out.

Everyone Has Attained Zen

Sixin Wuxin (1043-1114) joined the assembly of Zen master Huitang Zuxin. While on pilgrimage he heard a clap of thunder and was enlightened; returning to Huitang, he said, "Everyone in the world has attained Zen, they just haven't realized it."

Te-shan's Ultimate Teaching

Hsueh-feng asked Te-shan, "Can I also share the ultimate teaching the old patriarchs attained?"

Te-shan hit him with a stick, saying, "What are you talking about?"

Hsueh-feng did not realize Te-shan's meaning, so the next day he repeated his question.

Te-shan answered, "Zen has no words, neither does it have anything to give."

Yen-tou heard about the dialogue and said, "Te-shan has an iron back-bone, but he spoils Zen with his soft words."

Hsueh-feng's Wooden Ball

One day Hsueh-feng began a lecture to the monks gathered around the little platform by rolling down a wooden ball.

Hsuan-sha went after the ball, picked it up and replaced it on the stand.

The Last Rap

Tangen had studied with Sengai since childhood. When he was twenty, he wanted to leave his teacher and visit others for comparative study, but Sengai would not permit this. Every time Tangen suggested it, Sengai would give him a rap on the head.

Finally Tangen asked an elder brother to coax permission from Sengai. This the brother did and then reported to Tangen: "It is arranged. I have fixed it for you start your pilgrimage at once."

Tangen went to Sengai to thank him for his permission. The master answered by giving him another rap.

When Tangen related this to his elder brother the other said: "What is the matter? Sengai has no business giving permission and then changing his mind. I will tell him so." And off he went to see the teacher.

"I did not cancel my permission," said Sengai. "I just wished to give him one last smack over the head, for when he returns, he will be enlightened, and I will not be able to reprimand him again."

Attainment

One day a monk asked Master Xuefeng, "When you visited your masters, what was it that you attained that put an end to your search?"

Xuefeng said, "I went with empty hands and I returned with empty hands."

Understand?

Zen Master Bajiao entered the hall and addressed the monks, saying, "Do you understand? Those who know are few. Take care."

The Most Profound Teaching

A monk asked, "What is the most profound teaching you offer?"

Zen Master Cuiyan called to his attendant, "Come and boil some tea!"

The First Principle

A monk asked, "What is the first principle?"

Zen Master Fayan said, "When I speak to you that is the second principle."

Just follow the flow.

Ta-mei Fa-chang (752-839) was a Chinese Ch'an master. After he got awakened under
the Great Master Ma-tsu Tao-i (709-788), he went to the Ta-mei mountain and resided there.

One day there was a traveling monk who got lost in the Ta-mei mountain and unexpectedly saw the Ch'an master. The monk asked:

-How long have you been here, Sir?

Fa-chang replied:

-I've only seen the green mountain turns into the yellow one.

The monk then asked:

-Would you please give me the direction to go out of this mountain?

Fa-chang replied:

-Just follow the flow.

Suiwo and the sound of one hand clapping

Suiwo, the disciple of Hakuin, was a good teacher. On a certain day a certain pupil came to him, and Suiwo gave him the problem, "Hear the sound of one hand."

The pupil remained three years, but could not pass the test. One night he came to Suiwo in tears. "I must return to my home in shame," he said, "for I cannot solve the problem."

"Wait another week," said Suiwo. "Meditate constantly." Still no enlightenment came to the pupil. "Try for another week," said Suiwo. The pupil obeyed, but to no avail.

"Still another week," requested Suiwo, but in vain. In despair the pupil begged to be released, but Suiwo asked for one more meditation of five days. They too were without result. Then Suiwo said: "Mediate for three days longer. If you still fail to attain enlightenment, you had better kill yourself."

On the second day the pupil was enlightened.

Why Didn't you Tell Me?

A monk who had studied under the Zen master Kassan for a period of time. Then he left him to go to many other places for more Zen enquiry. However, he could not find any place that fitted him. Furthermore, at any place visited, he hread that Kassan was praised as one of the great Zen masters. Therefore, the monk was back with Kassan and asked him: "At any place I visited, it was said that you, Sir, have very deep understanding, why didn't you tell me about that?"
Kassan replied: "When you started to cook, I kindled the fire. When you shared the food,
I gave you my bowl. Was there any time I disappointed you?"
Right under the words, the monk awaked.

Wonder of Wonders

Student: "Is there anything more miraculous than the wonders of nature?"

Zen Master: "Yes. Your appreciation of these wonders."

~ Encyclopedia of Spirituality ~
~ Timothy Freke ~

The Ancient Saying

Once a monk coming to question Master Xuefeng began to say, "The ancients had a saying..."

The master immediately lay down. After a while he got up and asked, "What were you saying?"

As the monk started to repeat the question, the master said, "Wasting your life; drowning in the waves."

The Question

A monk asked, "If one wants to reach the road of no life and death, one must first see the original source. What is the original source?"

Zen Master Baofu Congzhan (860?-928) was silent for a long while. Then he said to his attendant, "What was it that that monk just asked me?"

The monk repeated his question.

Baofu yelled, "I'm not deaf!"

The Artist

A non-Buddhist presented Hogen with a screen that had a picture painted on it. When he had finished looking at it, Hogen said, "Did you paint this with your hand or your mind?"
The artist answered, "With my mind."
Hogen said, "What is this mind of yours?"
The artist had no answer.

~ Osho: Zen, The Quantum Leap from Mind to No-Mind ~

Myosho

Myosho was a disciple of Razan. At his first meeting with Razan, he jumped to his feet as soon as he had made his bows, and Razan asked him where he had come from. By way of answer, Myosho asked, "What is it that is happening just at this moment?"

Razan saluted him graciously, and said, "Have some tea!"

Myosho hesitated, and Razan said, "It's a warm autumn day; why don't you go out somewhere?"

Myosho sighed and thought that he had started off full of ambition, and it had all come to this, to nothing.

The next day he tried again, but Razan said, "The feathers are not fully grown, and the wings are not strong enough yet; go away!"

Afterwards, when he was enlightened, Myosho did not stay in one spot, but went round the country converting all kinds of people.

Forty years later, when he was about to die, Myosho ascended the rostrum and admonished and instructed the monks. That evening he stretched out his legs and said to the monk-attendant, "Long ago, Shaka Nyorai stretched out both legs, and a hundred treasures of glorious light were emitted. Tell me, aren't I emitting some?"

The attendant replied, "In ancient times, the crane grove; today, your honor!"

Myosho rumpled his eyebrows and said, "Isn't some fox making a fool of me?" He then recited a gatha, sat in the proper way and quietly and slowly passed away.

~ Osho: Zen, The Solitary Bird, Cuckoo of The Forest ~

Way Without Mistakes

A monk asked Joshu, "What is the way without mistakes?"
Joshu said, "Knowing one's mind, seeing into one's nature,
is the way without mistakes."

~ Osho: Zen, The Solitary Bird, Cuckoo of The Forest ~

Shock

The Japanese Master Ekido was a severe teacher and his pupils feared him.

One day, as one of his pupils was striking the time of day on the temple gong, he missed a beat because he was watching a beautiful girl who was passing the gates.

Unknown to the pupil, Ekido was standing behind him. Ekido struck the pupil with his staff, and the shock stopped the heart of the pupil, and he died.

Because the old custom of the pupil signing his life over to the master had sunk to a mere formality, Ekido was discredited by the general public.

But after this incident, Ekido produced ten enlightened successors, an unusually high number.

~ Osho: A Bird On The Wing ~

Sacrilege

One winter day, a masterless samurai came to Eisai's temple and made an appeal: 'I'm poor and sick,' he said, 'and my family is dying of hunger. Please help us, master.'

Dependent as he was on widows' mites, Eisai's life was very austere, and he had nothing to give.

He was about to send the samurai off when he remembered the image of Yakushi-buddha in the hall. Going up to it he tore off its halo and gave it to the samurai. 'Sell this,' said Eisai, 'it should tide you over.' The bewildered but desperate samurai took the halo and left.

'Master!' cried one of Eisai's disciples, 'that's sacrilege! How could you do such a thing?'

'Sacrilege? Bah! I have merely put the buddha's mind, which is full of love and mercy, to use, so to speak. Indeed, if he himself had heard that poor samurai he'd have cut off a limb for him.'

~ Osho: Ancient Music in The Pines ~

A Common Disease

By surrounding himself with true believers, Waldo fell into the trap of taking himself too seriously. This led to unhappiness and ill health. When he asked Ralph, one of the few who had penetrated his multilevel cover stories, what he thought the problems was, Ralph replied, "You're suffering from hardening of the orthodoxies."

~ Zen Without Zen Masters by Camden Benares ~

Sentenced to Death

A Zen monk was sentenced to death.

The king of the country called him and said to him, "You have only twenty-four hours - how are you going to live them?"

The monk laughed and said, "Moment to moment - as I have always lived!

There has never been more than this moment for me, so what does it matter whether I have twenty-four hours or twenty-four years?

It is irrelevant.

I have always lived moment to moment so one moment is more than enough for me.

Twenty-four hours is too much - one moment is quite enough.

The king could not understand it.

The monk said, "Let me ask you, sir: can you live two moments simultaneously?"

No one ever has. The only possible way to live is one moment at a time. Two moments are not given to you simultaneously; only one moment is ever in your hand. And that one moment is so flickering that if you are engrossed in the past or

enchanted by the future you will not be able to catch it.
It will pass you by and you will miss it.
Only the mind which is receptive, here and now, can create
the situation in which meditation happens.

~ Osho: The Silent Explosion ~

The Story of Thera Tissa

The Buddha uttered Verse (205) of Dhammapada at Vesali, with reference to Thera Tissa.

When the Buddha declared that in four months' time, he would realize **parinibbāna**, many puthujjana (worldly) monks were apprehensive. They were at a loss and did not know what to do, and so they kept close to the Buddha. But Thera Tissa, having resolved that he would attain arahatship in the life-time of the Buddha did not go to him, but left for a secluded place to practise meditation. Other bhikkhus, not understanding his behaviour, took him to the Buddha and said, "Venerable Sir, this bhikkhu does not seem to cherish and honour you; he only keeps to himself instead of coming to your presence." Thera Tissa then explained to them that he was striving hard to attain arahatship before the Buddha realized **parinibbāna**, and that was the only reason why he had not come to see the Buddha.

Having heard his explanation, the Buddha said to the bhikkhus, *"Bhikkhus! Those who love and respect me should act like Tissa. You are not paying homage to me by just offering me*

flowers, perfumes and incense. You pay homage to me only by practising the Lokuttara Dhamma, i.e., Insight Meditation."
Then the Buddha spoke in verse as follows:

Pavivekarasam pitvā
rasam upasamassa ca
niddaro hoti nippāpo
dhammapitirasam pivam
"Having had the taste of solitude and the taste of Perfect Peace of Nibbana, one who drinks in the joy of the essence of the Dhamma is free from fear and evil."
[Dhammapada, Verse 205]

At the end of the discourse Thera Tissa attained Sotapatti Fruition.

No Knowledge

A monk asked, "What is a man of no knowledge?"
Zen Master Joshu said, "What are you talking about?"

This

A student once went to a famous Zen master with the following question:

"If someone were to ask me a hundred years from now what I thought was your deepest understanding, what should I say?" The master replied: "Tell them I said, 'It is simply This!'"

The Prince

In China there was once a Prince who loved birds. Whenever he found an injured bird, he would feed and nurse it back to health; and then, when the bird had regained its strength, he would set it free with much rejoicing.

Naturally, he grew quite famous for his talent as a loving healer of wounded birds. Whenever an injured bird was found anywhere in his kingdom, the bird would quickly be brought to him, and he would express his gratitude to the thoughtful person who brought it.

But then, in order to curry the Prince's favor, people soon began to catch birds and to deliberately injure them so that they could take them to the palace.

So many birds were killed in the course of capture and maiming that his kingdom became a hell for birds.

When the Prince saw how much harm

his goodness was causing, he decreed that no wounded bird should ever be helped.

When people saw that there was no profit to be gained from helping birds, they ceased harming them.

Sometimes it happens that our experiences are like this Prince's. Sometimes, when we think we're doing the most good, we learn to our chagrin that we're actually causing the most harm.

~ Zen Master Xu Yun ~

Perfection

One day, the priest was told that important guests were expected. Immediately, he set about tending the garden. He removed weeds, pruned tree branches and shrubs. He even combed the moss! Since it was autumn, the ground was untidy with dry leaves which the priest painstakingly raked and arranged into neat mounds.

All this while, the old monk was watching him from across the wall. The priest finished with his labor of love. A look of satisfaction spread across his face. "Doesn't it look beautiful now?" he said, turning to the monk.

"Indeed, it does," replied the monk, "but something's not quite right. Here, give me a hand over this wall and I'll fix it for you."

Puzzled, the priest did as he was asked. The old master made his way slowly to a tree in the center of the garden, gripped its trunk and shook it hard. Leaves scattered down, orange, russet and brown. "There...that's better! Now, can you help me back across the wall?"

Perfection is....not always what you think it is!

Your Light May Go Out

A student of Tendai, a philosophical school of Buddhism, came to the Zen abode of Gasan as a pupil. When he was departing a few years later, Gasan warned him: "Studying the truth speculatively is useful as a way of collecting preaching material. But remember that unless you meditate constantly your light of truth may go out."

The Buddha In the Home

One day, a young man named Yang fu left his parents to go to Sichuan (Szechwan) to visit the bodhisattva Wuji.

He met a Zen Master in the way who asked, "Where are you going young man?"

Yang Fu said, "I am going to study under Wuji the bodhisattva."

"Instead of looking for a mere bodhisattva, you'd be better off looking for the Buddha."

"Do you know where I can find the Buddha?"

"When you return home, a person wearing a blanket and with shoes on the wrong feet will come to greet you. That person is the Buddha."

"Really?"

Yang fu hurried back. Arriving at his home late at night. In her joyful haste to greet her returning son Yang fu's mother three on a blanket and accidentally put her slippers on the wrong feet. Yang fu took one look at her and was suddenly enlightened.

Because I'm Here

An old monk was sweeping the yard in a monastery under the scorching sun.

Another monk passed by and asked him, "How old are you?"

The old monk replied, "I'm seventy-seven."

"You are so old! Why are you still working so hard here?"

"Well, because I'm here."

"But why are you working under the scorching sun?"

"Because the sun is there."

The Perfect Question

A monk asked, "What is the perfect question?"
Zen Master Joshu said, "Wrong!"

Shiwu's Enlightenment

Monk Shiwu or Stonehouse (1272–1352) is said to have followed a monk to the Tienmu Mountains to meet with Chan master Kao-Feng. On his arrival Kao-feng asked why he came to his hermitage to which Shiwu answered "I've come for the Dharma".

Kao-feng said "The Dharma isn't so easy to find. You've got to burn your fingers for incense".

Shiwu replied "But I see the Master before me with my own eyes. How could the Dharma be hidden?".

Kao-feng took him as his pupil and gave him the koan "All things return to one" for study.

After three years with little progress, Shiwu decided to leave and Kao-feng recommended he study under the Chan master Chi-an. Shiwu crossed the Yangtze and met Chi-an at West Peak Temple near Chienyang.

Chi-an asked Shiwu what teaching he had received.

Shiwu said, "All things return to one".

Chi-an asked what it meant and Shiwu remained silent.

Chi-an said "Those words are dead. Where did you pick up such rot?".

Shiwu bowed and asked for instruction.

Chi-an then gave him another koan: "Where buddhas dwell, don't stop. Where buddhas don't dwell, hurry past".

Shiwu said he didn't understand but decided to stay with Chi-an.

One day, Chi-an asked once more about the koan and Shiwu answered, "When you mount the horse, you see the road".

Chi-an admonished him once again.

Shiwu left but on his way down the mountain he saw a pavilion and had a sudden insight. He turned back and told Chi-an, "Where buddhas dwell, don't stop. Those are dead words. Where buddhas don't dwell, hurry past. Those are dead words too. Now I understand living words".

Chi-an asked him what he understood and Shiwu answered, "When the rain finally stops in late spring, the oriole appears on a branch."

Chi-an later served as abbot of the Taochang temple and Shiwu joined him. Shiwu also served as a meditation teacher in Lingyin temple.

Sitting alone in a quiet room

The great Zen Master Dao-an [1312-1385] sat alone in a quiet room for twelve years, exerting his spirit to the utmost in contemplation: only then did he attain spiritual awakening.

Sitting in a tree hanging over a cliff

Zen teacher Jinglin gave up lecturing on the sutras to practice Zen, but drowsiness disturbed his mind. There was a precipitous cliff with a thousand-foot drop, with a tree projecting out over it. Jinglin tied himself to this tree with a rope of plaited straw, and sat cross-legged in the treetop.

He wholeheartedly focused his mind, and sat there day and night. Such was his fear of death in such a precarious position, that he was able to concentrate his spirit single-mindedly. Later he experienced transcendent awakening.

The Liar Buddha

If a Buddha would not speak, then people would have no hope of liberation; but if a Buddha speaks, then people pursue the words and create interpretations, so there would be little advantage and much disadvantage. That is why the Buddha said, "I would rather not explain the truth, but enter into extinction right away."

But then afterward he thought back on all the Buddhas of the past, who had all taught the doctrines of three vehicles. After that he made temporary use of verses to explain, and provisionally established names and terms.

Originally it is not Buddha, but he told people, "This is Buddha." Originally it is not enlightenment, but he told people, "This is enlightenment, peace, liberation," and so on. He knew people couldn't bear a burden of ten thousand pounds, so for the time being he taught them the incomplete teaching. And he realized the spread of good ways, which was still better than evil ways.

But when the limits of good results are fulfilled, then bad consequences ensue. Once you have "Buddha," then there are sentient beings." Once you have "nirvana," then there is "birth and death." Once you have light, then there is darkness. As long as cause and effect with attachment continue to operate, there is nothing that does not have consequences.

~ Zen Master Baizhang Huaihai (720-814) ~

At a Funeral Procession

At the funeral of one of his monks, as the Abbot joined the procession, Zen Master Joshu remarked, "What a long procession of dead bodies follows the wake of a single living person!"

No Teaching?

Master Tenno was asked by a monk: 'I have been with you for three years, and received no teaching from you. Why?'

The Master said: 'Have I not been teaching you ever since you arrived?'

'When did you give me any teaching!' asked the monk.

Master Tenno said: 'When you brought me tea, I received it from you. When you bowed to me, I inclined my head to you. When did I not teach you?'

While the monk was still pondering this, Master Tenno added: 'When you look, just look. If you wonder about it, you won't get to the point.'

On this, the monk awakened.

~ The Wisdom of the Zen masters ~
~ Irmgard Schloegl ~

One Road

Question: What is the one road of Yun-men?
Zen Master Yun-men: Personal-experience!

Understanding of Buddha

A monk asked, "If someone is seeking an understanding of Buddha, what's the best path to doing so?"

Zen Master Fayan Wenyi (885-958) said, "It doesn't pass here."

Advanced Student

A monk asked, "What is the thing toward which an advanced student should pay particular attention?"

Zen Master Fayan Wenyi (885-958) said, "If the student has anything whatsoever that is particular then he can't be called advanced."

The Ultimate Teaching

A monk asked, "What is the ultimate teaching of all Buddhas?"

Zen Master Fayan Wenyi (885-958) said, "You have it too."

Auspicious Sign

A monk asked the Master Ch'u-hui Chen-chi as he appeared for the first time as an abbot, "I hear that when Shakyamuni began his public life, golden lotus sprang from the earth. Today, at the inauguration of Your Reverence, what auspicious sign may we expect?"

The new Abbot said, "I have just swept away the snow before the gate."

~ The Golden Age of Zen ~

Words of Ancient

A monk asked, "What are the words of the ancients?"
Zen Master Joshu said, "Listen carefully! Listen carefully!"

One Word

A monk asked, "What is one word?"
Zen Master Joshu said, "Two words."

~ Case 257 of The Recorded Sayings of Zen Master Joshu
~
~ Translated by James Green ~

Finding a Piece of the Truth

One day Mara, the Evil One, was travelling through a village with his attendants. He saw a man doing walking meditation whose face was lit up on wonder. The man had just discovered something on the ground in front of him. Mara's attendant asked what that was, and Mara replied, "A piece of truth."

"Doesn't this bother you when someone finds a piece of truth, O Evil One?" his attendant asked.

"No," Mara replied. "Right after this, they usually make a belief out of it."

Archery

A Zen Master observing students at archery practice notices one of them who is consistently missing the mark, and says: "It is his desire to win that drains him of power."

Moving to a New City

There was a person coming to a new village, relocating, and he was wondering if he would like it there, so he went to a Zen master and asked: Do you think I will like it in this village? Are the people nice?

The master asked back: How were the people on the town where you come from? "They were nasty and greedy, they were angry and lived for cheating and stealing," said the newcomer.

"Those are exactly the type of people we have in this village," said the master.

Another newcomer to the village visited the master and asked the same question, to which the master asked: How were the people in the town where you come from? "They were sweet and lived in harmony, they cared for one another and for the land, they respected each other and they were seekers of spirit," he replied.

"Those are exactly the type of people we have in this village," said the master!

Flow Like A River

There is the story of a young martial arts student who was under the tutelage of a famous master.

One day, the master was watching a practice session in the courtyard. He realized that the presence of the other students was interfering with the young man's attempts to perfect his technique.

The master could sense the young man's frustration. He went up to the young man and tapped him on his shoulder.

"What's the problem?" he inquired.

"I don't know", said the youth, with a strained expression.

"No matter how much I try, I am unable to execute the moves properly".

"Before you can master technique, you must understand harmony. Come with me, I will explain", replied the master.

The teacher and student left the building and walked some distance into the woods until they came upon a stream. The master stood silently on the bank for several moments. Then he spoke.

"Look at the stream," he said. "There are rocks in its way. Does it slam into them out of frustration? It simply flows over and around them and moves on! Be like the water and you will know what harmony is."

The young man took the master's advice to heart. Soon, he was barely noticing the other students around him. Nothing could come in his way of executing the most perfect moves.

The Meditating Man

A serious young man found the conflicts of mid-20th Century America confusing. He went to many people seeking a way of resolving within himself the discords that troubled him, but he remained troubled.

One night in a coffee house, a self-ordained Zen Master said to him, "Go to the dilapidated mansion you will find at this address which I have written down for you. Do not speak to those who live there; you must remain silent until the moon rises tomorrow night. Go to the large room on the right of the main hallway, sit in the lotus position on top of the rubble in the northeast corner, face the corner, and meditate."

He did as the Zen Master instructed. His meditation was frequently interrupted by worries. He worried whether the rest of the plumbing fixtures would fall from the second-floor bathroom to join the pipes and other trash he was sitting on. He worried how would he know when the moon rose on the next night. He worried about what the people who walked through the room said about him.

His worrying and meditation were disturbed when, as if in a test of faith, ordure (some dirty substance) fell from the second floor onto him. At that time two people walked into the room. The first asked the second who the man sitting there was. The second replied "Some say he is a holy man; Others say he is a shithead."

Hearing this, the man was enlightened.

The Painting

Once upon a time there was a Shogun who wanted a nice picture of a chicken to go in his tokonoma.

So, he went to a very fine artist (Hiroshige? Sharaku?) and said, "I want you to paint me the best picture of a chicken that you can."

So, the artist said, "Hai, hai, mochiron, kore o shimasu." (Yes, yes, certainly, I will do this.)

The artist went to his cabin high on Mount Fuji. He brought books of bird anatomy, many studies of birds done by all the famous artists of the past, He sculpted chickens, he painted chickens in oil, he did one woodblock after another of nothing but chickens. He depicted chickens in bushido poses, crashing through the shoji in a samurai palace. He drew noble portraits of chickens in virtuous attitudes. He used a sumie brush to catch every nuance of a chicken's life. He painted chickens in the landscape and in the boudoir, on the battle-field and in the barn.

Ten years passed.

One day the shogun was at archery practice when he thought of his request to the artist. He immediately mounted his steed and made his way to the artist's cabin. It was hard to enter the door. There were sketches of chickens stacked to the ceiling. There were statues of chickens everywhere. There were skeletons of chickens and paintings of chickens. There was nowhere to sit and very little space to stand.

"Where is my chicken drawing?" demanded the Shogun.

"Oh," said the artist, "I forgot, sorry." And he took a brush, whirled it very quickly on a piece of rice paper, handed the paper to the Shogun, and said, "Here."

The Donkey

A man's favorite donkey falls into a deep precipice. He can't pull it out no matter how hard he tries. He therefore decides to bury it alive.

Soil is poured onto the donkey from above. The donkey feels the load, shakes it off, and steps on it. More soil is poured.

It shakes it off and steps up. The more the load was poured, the higher it rose. By noon, the donkey was grazing in green pastures.

After much shaking off (of problems) And stepping up (learning from them), One will graze in GREEN PASTURES.

The Obstacle

There once was a very wealthy and curious king. This king had a huge boulder placed in the middle of a road. Then he hid nearby to see if anyone would try to remove the gigantic rock from the road.

The first people to pass by were some of the king's wealthiest merchants and courtiers. Rather than moving it, they simply walked around it. A few loudly blamed the King for not maintaining the roads. Not one of them tried to move the boulder.

Finally, a peasant came along. His arms were full of vegetables. When he got near the boulder, rather than simply walking around it as the others had, the peasant put down his load and tried to move the stone to the side of the road. It took a lot of effort but he finally succeeded.

The peasant gathered up his load and was ready to go on his way when he say a purse lying in the road where the boulder had been. The peasant opened the purse. The purse was stuffed full of gold coins and a note from the king. The king's note said the purse's gold was a reward for moving the boulder from the road.

The king showed the peasant what many of us never understand: every obstacle presents an opportunity to improve our condition.

Bad Temper

There once was a little boy who had a bad temper. His father gave him a bag of nails and told him that every time he lost his temper, he must hammer a nail into the back of the fence.

The first day, the boy had driven 37 nails into the fence. Over the next few weeks, as he learned to control his anger, the number of nails hammered daily gradually dwindled down. He discovered it was easier to hold his temper than to drive those nails into the fence.

Finally, the day came when the boy didn't lose his temper at all. He told his father about it and the father suggested that the boy now pull out one nail for each day that he was able to hold his temper. The days passed and the boy was finally able to tell his father that all the nails were gone.

The father took his son by the hand and led him to the fence. He said, "You have done well, my son, but look at the holes in the fence. The fence will never be the same. When you say things in anger, they leave a scar just like this one. You can put a knife in a man and draw it out. It won't matter how many times you say I'm sorry. The wound is still there."

Ordinary

A monk said, "I don't have a special question. Please don't give a special reply."

Zen Master Joshu said, "How extraordinary."

Let Go

A man visited a great mystic to find out how to let go of his chains of attachment and his prejudices. Instead of answering him directly, the mystic jumped to his feet and bolted to a nearby pillar, flung his arms around it, grasping the marble surface as he screamed, "Save me from this pillar! Save me from this pillar!"

The man who had asked the question could not believe what he saw. He thought the mystic was mad. The shouting soon brought a crowd of people. "Why are you doing that?" the man asked. "I came to you to ask a spiritual question because I thought you were wise, but obviously, you're crazy. **You** are holding the pillar; the pillar is not holding you. You can simply let go."

The mystic let go of the pillar and said to the man, "If you can understand that, you have your answer. Your chains of attachment are not holding you, you are holding them. You can simply let go."

Expression

A Zen monk was with his roshi one day when the roshi was murdered by thieves. His roshi cried out in fear and pain as he was being murdered, and this disturbed the student greatly. He was about to leave the monastery when another roshi approached him and said, "Fool! The object of Zen is not to suppress all emotion, but to free us to fully express at the appropriate moment."

Emotion

A Zen story concerns an elder monk in a Japanese monastery. The young novices were in awe of this man, not because he was severe with them, but because nothing ever seemed to upset him. A few of the young men decided to test the monk by devising a plan to scare him.

Early one dark winter morning, it was the monk's duty to carry tea to the Founders Hall. The young men hid in the alcove of a long and winding corridor near the entrance to the hall. Just as the monk passed, they rushed out screaming like crazy men. Without faltering a step, the monk continued walking on quietly, carefully carrying the tea. When he arrived at his destination, he set down the tray, covered the tea bowl so no dust could fall into it and then fell back against the wall and cried out in shock "Oh-oh-oh!"

A Zen Master relating this story said, "There is nothing wrong with emotions. Only one must not let them carry one away or interfere with what one is doing."

Dedication

A Zen story tells of two monks who met on the road. After their initial greetings, one monk asked the other, "What are you going to do tonight, my friend?" The second monk replied, "I will meditate and pray in the temple. What are you going to do?" "I'm going to spend a night of pleasure with the ladies," he answered.

The monks then went on their own ways, and that night in the house of pleasure, the monk was quite distracted. All he could think about was his friend meditating and praying. But was the other monk at peace with himself? No, he continued to think about his friend enjoying an evening with women.

When you make a choice, accept it completely and surrender to all the experiences that go along with your decision.

Attention

A Zen student asked his **Roshi** the most important element of Zen.

The **Roshi** replied, "Attention." "Yes, thank you," the student replied. "But can you tell me the second most important element?"

And the **Roshi** replied, "Attention."

The Sound of the Bell

A little boy from a small village was taken by bandits. They put a sack over him, and he couldn't see anything. As they were taking him away from his home, he heard the sound of the church bell; it got dimmer and dimmer as he was carried further and further him away.

When he grew up, he managed to escape from his captors. But he had nowhere to go as he had no clue as to where or in what country his home and family were. The only thing he vaguely remembered was the sound of a bell. He instinctively walked, passing to village after village, working for a few days, then moving on. He heard many many bells, but he knew inside that the sound wasn't the same. He continued, always listening for that bell.

Eventually he was fed up with the years of wondering and wanted to end it all. Then he heard a dim sound, he knew it was the same bell he heard inside his head all those years ago; he walked and then ran towards it. He asked the villagers if they knew of a family whose boy had been abducted 30 years ago. They did know of one, and they took him to his home.

Enlightened

One day the Master announced that a young monk had reached an advanced state of enlightenment. The news caused some stir. Some of the monks went to see the young monk. "We heard you are enlightened. Is that true?" they asked.

"It is," he replied.

"And how do you feel?"

"As miserable as ever," said the monk.

Tea Combat

A master of the tea ceremony in old Japan once accidentally slighted a soldier. He quickly apologized, but the rather impetuous soldier demanded that the matter be settled in a sword duel. The tea master, who had no experience with swords, asked the advice of a fellow Zen master who did possess such skill. As he was served by his friend, the Zen swordsman could not help but notice how the tea master performed his art with perfect concentration and tranquility. "Tomorrow," the Zen swordsman said, "when you duel the soldier, hold your weapon above your head, as if ready to strike, and face him with the same concentration and tranquility with which you perform the tea ceremony." The next day, at the appointed time and place for the duel, the tea master followed this advice. The soldier, readying himself to strike, stared for a long time into the fully attentive but calm face of the tea master. Finally, the soldier lowered his sword, apologized for his arrogance, and left without a blow being struck.

True Self

A distraught man approached the Zen master. "Please, Master, I feel lost, desperate. I don't know who I am. Please, show me my true self!" But the teacher just looked away without responding. The man began to plead and beg, but still the master gave no reply. Finally giving up in frustration, the man turned to leave. At that moment, the master called out to him by name. "Yes!" the man said as he spun back around. "There it is!" exclaimed the master.

The Strange Advice

A novice once went to a Zen Master to ask his advice on how best to become enlightened. 'Go to the cemetery and insult the dead,' said the master.

The brother did as he was told. The following day, he went back to the master. 'Did they respond?' asked the master.

'No,' said the novice.

'Then go and praise them instead.'

The novice obeyed. That same afternoon, he went back to the master, who again asked if the dead had responded.

'No, they didn't,' said the novice.

'In order to become enlightened, do exactly as they did,' master told him.

'Take no notice of men's scorn or of their praise; in that way, you will be able to build your own path.'

The Ultimate Teaching

A monk asked, "What is the ultimate teaching of all Buddhas?"

Zen Master Fayan Wenyi (885-958) said, "You have it too."

Fees

A Zen Master spent his whole life teaching that all the answers to our questions are in ourselves, but his congregation insisted on consulting him about everything they did.

One day, the master had an idea. He placed a notice on the door of his house, saying: 'ANSWERS TO QUESTIONS – 1000 YEN PER ANSWER.'

A shopkeeper decided to pay the one thousand yens. He gave the rabbi the money and said: 'Don't you think that's rather a lot to charge for a question?'

'Yes, I do,' said the master. 'And I have just answered your question. If you want to know anything else, you'll have to pay another one thousand yens, or else look for the answer inside yourself, which is far cheaper and much more efficient.'

From then on, no one bothered him.

Life

"What is it you seek?" asked the Master of a scholar who came to him for guidance.

"Life." was the reply.

Said the Master, "If you are to live, words must die." When asked later what he meant, he said.

"You are lost and forlorn because you dwell in a world of words. You feed on words you are satisfied with words when what you need is substance. A menu will not satisfy your hunger. A formula will not slake your thirst. "

Supernatural Powers of Buddha

Master Rinzai in a sermon to his monk's quotes from the scriptures that the Buddha has supernatural powers and explains what they are. What we usually call supernatural powers are not the Buddha's. After all the demon king on losing a battle made his whole host of fiends, 84,000 of them, vanish in the hollow stalk of a lotus. Would that make the demon king a Buddha? The Buddha's supernatural powers are the true ones, and only a Buddha possesses them: seeing without being deceived by colour and form, hearing without being deceived by sound, smelling without being deceived by smells, tasting without being deceived by tastes, touching without being deceived by touch, and thinking without being deceived by mental configurations.

~ The Wisdom of the Zen masters ~
~ Irmgard Schloegl ~

Who are you?

When the Buddha start to wander around India shortly after his enlightenment, he encountered several men who recognized him to be a very extraordinary being.

They asked him, "Are you a god?"

"No," he replied.

"Are you a reincarnation of god?"

"No," he replied.

"Are you a wizard, then?"

"No."

"Well, are you a man?"

"No."

"So, what are you?" they asked, being very perplexed.

"I am awake."

Buddha means "The Awakened One". How to awaken is all he taught.

The Mustard Seeds

Kisa Gotami was the wife of a wealthy man of Savatthi. She had only one child. When her son was old enough to start running about, he caught a disease and died. Kisa Gotami was greatly saddened. Unable to accept that her son was dead and could not be brought back to life again, she took him in her arms and went about asking for medicine to cure him. Everyone she encountered thought that she had lost her mind. Finally, an old man told her that if there was anyone who could help her, it would be the Buddha.

In her distress, Kisa Gotami brought the body of her son to the Buddha and asked him for a medicine that would bring back his life. The Buddha answered: "I shall cure him if you can bring me some mustard seeds from a house where no one has died". Carrying her dead son, she went from door to door, asking at each house. At each house the reply was always that someone had died there. At last the truth struck her, "No house is free from death". She laid the body of her child in the wood and returned to the Buddha, who comforted her and preached to her the truth. She was awakened and entered the first stage of Arhatship. Eventually, she became an Arhat.

You Are Also Correct

Two monks who came out of a lecture by their master went on a hot debate regarding what they heard during the lecture. Each of them insisted that his understanding was the correct one. To settle the dispute, they went to see the master for a judgement.

After hearing the argument put forth by the first monk, the master said, "You are correct!" The monk was overjoyed. Casting a winner's glance at his friend, he left the room.

The second monk was upset and started to pour out what he thought to the master. After he finished, the master looked at him and said, "You are correct, too." Hearing this, the second monk brightened up and went away.

A third monk who was also in the room was greatly puzzled by what he saw. He said to the master, "I am confused, master! Their positions regarding the issue are completely opposite. They can't be both right! How could you say that they are both correct?"

The master smiled as he looked into the eyes of this third monk, "You are also correct!"

The Entrance to Zen

A monk was anxious to learn Zen and said, "I have been newly initiated into the Brotherhood and will you be gracious enough to show me the way to Zen?"

The master said, "Do you hear the murmuring sound of the mountain stream?"

The monk answered, "Yes, I do."

The master said, "Here is the entrance."

The Truth

A lay disciple who was a follower of Zen master Yakusan asked: "What is the truth?"

Yakusan pointed up and down.

"Have you got it?"

But the disciple could not understand: "No."

Then Yakusan added: "Cloud in the blue sky, water in the jar."

The disciple was suddenly enlightened.

Prajna

Chao-chou Ts'ung-shen went to visit T'ou-tzu Ta-t'ung and asked, "What is the substance of prajna?" T'ou-tzu repeated, "What is the substance of prajna?"

Thereupon Chao-chou laughed heartily and left.

Next morning, when T'ou-tzu saw Chao-chou sweeping the yard, he stepped forward, and asked, "What is the substance of prajna?" As soon as Chao-chou heard this, he threw down his broom, and laughing heartily, went away.

Muzhou's Great Matter

Muzhou, while instructing the assembly, said, "When the great matter has not been completed, this is like mourning one's dead parents. When the great matter has been completed, this is like mourning one's dead parents."

Same or Different?

Question: "Are the teachings of Buddha and the teachings of the Patriarch [Bodhidharma] the same?"
Zen master Mu-chou Tao-tsung: "A green mountain is a green mountain, and white clouds are white clouds."

The Beyond

Chao-chou asked (his master) Nan-ch'uan, "Please tell me what it is that goes beyond the four alternatives and the hundredfold negations." Nan-ch'uan made no answer but went to his room.

Where?

A monk asked, "Where are one's nostrils before one is born?"

Zen Master Nansen replied, "Where are one's nostrils after one has been born?"

Avyakrit

Potthapada: "Is it the case that the cosmos is eternal, that only this is true, and anything otherwise is worthless?"

Buddha: "Potthapada, I haven't expounded that the cosmos is eternal, that only this is true, and anything otherwise is worthless. It is a matter about which I have expressed no opinion."

"Then is it the case that the cosmos is not eternal, that only this is true, and anything otherwise is worthless?"

"Potthapada, I haven't expounded that the cosmos is not eternal, that only this is true, and anything otherwise is worthless. It is a matter about which I have expressed no opinion."

[Potthapada goes on asking similar questions and Buddha goes on replying similarly:]

"Then is it the case that the cosmos is finite... the cosmos is infinite... the soul & the body are the same... the soul is one thing and the body another... after death a Tathagata exists... after death a Tathagata does not exist... after death a Tathagata both exists & does not exist... after death a Tathagata neither exists nor does not exist, that only this is true, and anything otherwise is worthless?"

"Potthapada, I haven't expounded that after death a Tathagata neither exists nor does not exist, that only this is true, and anything otherwise is worthless."

"But why hasn't the Blessed One expounded these things?"

"Because they are not conducive to the goal, are not conducive to the Dhamma, are not basic to the holy life. They don't lead to disenchantment, to dispassion, to cessation, to calm, to direct knowledge, to self-awakening, to Unbinding. That's why I haven't expounded them."

"Then what has Blessed One expressed an opinion about?"

"Potthapada, I have taught what dukkha is; I have taught what is the origin of dukkha; I have taught what is the cessation of dukkha; I have taught the method by which one can reach the cessation of dukkha."

"And why has the Blessed One taught this?"

"Because, Potthapada, this is profitable; it is concerned with the Dhamma, it leads to right conduct, to disenchantment, to dispassion, to calm, to tranquility, to higher knowledge, to the insights [of the higher stages of the Path], to Nibbana. Therefore, Potthapada, I have taught this."

" So it is, Blessed One. So it is, O One Well-gone. And now let the Blessed One do what seems fit to him."

And the Blessed One rose from his seat and departed.

~ Potthapada Sutta of Digha Nikaya of Sutta Pitaka ~

The Strange Monk

Once when Zen Master Kuei-shan complained that his disciples had not attained great action, one of his disciples, Chiu-feng Tzu-hui, stepped out of the crowd and started to walk away. When Kueishan called to him, he proceeded straight ahead without even turning his head. Kuei-shan remarked, "This man is certainly qualified to be a man of Ch'an."

Who is That Person?

Yung-a Chuan-teng said to his assembly, "There is a certain person, who avers, 'I do not depend on the blessing and help of the Buddha, I do not live in any of the three realms, I do not belong to the world of the five elements. The Patriarchs have not dared to pin me down, nor have the Buddha dared to give me a definite name.' Can you tell me who is that Person?"

Wu-hsieh Ling-meh, a disciple of Shih-t'ou as well as of Ma-tsu, was once asked by a monk, "What is greater than the heaven-and-earth?"
He replied, "No man can know him!"

~ The Golden Age of Zen ~

Impossible

A monk once came to Master Yung-ming Yen-shou and asked why, when he had been at the monastery for so long, he still did not understand the spirit of Yung-ming's teaching. "You should understand what is not to be understood," the Master answered. "How can I understand what is not to be understood?" pressed the monk. "From the womb of a cow an elephant is born; in the middle of the blue sea red dust is blown up," replied the Master.

The Fundamental Teaching

Monk: "What is the fundamental idea of the way of awakening?"

Yun-men: "When spring comes, the grass turns green of itself."

Distinguish

A monk asked Hsing-hua: 'I am unable to distinguish black from white. Pray enlighten me somehow.' The question was hardly out when the master gave him a good slashing.

Knowledge

'As to worldly knowledge and logical cleverness, I have nothing to do with them; pray let me have a Zen theme.' When this was asked by anmonk, the master gave him a hearty blow.

The Instruction

A monk said to Yün-mên, 'What would one do when no boundaries are seen, however wide the eyes are open?'
Said Yün-mên, 'Look!'

What is it?

When Nanyue [Huairang] first visited the sixth ancestor [Dajian Huineng], the ancestor asked him, "Where are you from?"

Nanyue said, "I came from the place of National Teacher Songshan [Hui]an.

The ancestor said, "What is this that thus comes?"

Nanyue never put this question aside. After eight years he told the sixth ancestor, "[I,] Huairang can now understand the question 'What is this that thus comes?' that you received me with upon my first arriving to see you."

The sixth ancestor said, "How do you understand it?"

Nanyue said, "To explain or demonstrate anything would miss the mark."

The sixth ancestor said, "Then do you suppose there is practice-realization or not?"

Nanyue said, "It is not that there is no practice-realization, but only that it cannot be defiled."

The sixth ancestor said, "This non-defilement is exactly what the buddhas protect and care for. I am thus, you are thus, and the ancestors in India also are thus."

~ Zen Master Dogen ~
~ Eihei Koroku ~

Deluded Thoughts

Whenever he received questions from students Chan master Fenzhou Wuye (760-821, disciple of Mazu Daoyi) often answered them by saying, "Do not have deluded thoughts."

Huanzhong Knows Illness

Chan master Huanzhong (780-862, disciple of Baizhang Huaihai) of Mt. Daci ascended the hall and said, "I do not know how to answer gongans (or koans). All I know is illness." At that time a certain monk stepped forward (to ask a question) and the master returned to the abbot's quarter.

Xuefeng's "Deliverance"

Xuefeng instructed the assembly, saying, "The worlds in all directions are the gate of deliverance, but if I hold your hand and drag you, you will not be allowed to enter." At that time a monk came forth and said, "Reverend, you suspect that I cannot (enter)." Another monk said, "What is the use of entering?" The master then hit him.

The Picked-Up Money

Once upon a time, there was a poor man who picked up a sack of money in the streets. He was overwhelmed with happiness. Then he began to count the money. Suddenly, the real owner of the money showed up. He had to give back the whole sack. He regretted for not having gone off to a faraway place sooner. He felt great pain for his loss.

Sore Eyes

Once upon a time, there was a woman who had a bad case of sore eyes. Another woman told her, "Where there are eyes, there are sometimes pains. Although my eyes do not ache now, I want to gouge them out so that they will not ache later."

A bystander said, "Though it's true that when you have your eyes, they may sometimes ache to disturb you, yet when you don't have them, you'll be sure to suffer for lifetime."

This is also held to be true with the common stupid men. People have heard that wealth and fame are the sources of decadence. They are afraid of retribution in the hereafter for not doing almsgiving in their present lives. The more wealth they have, the more troubles they sometimes suffer afterwards. It is said that if you do almsgiving, you may be happy, or you may be not. But if you don't do it, you will surely be the most unhappy man.

This is just like that woman who could not bear the thought of having sore eyes, wanted to gouge them out to suffer forever.

To Milk a Donkey

Once upon a time, there was a group of frontiersmen who had never seen a donkey before. Thus, they could not identify it. They were told that its milk was delicious. It happened that they found a male donkey and they tried to milk it. They began their wrangling about apprehending it.

One seized its head: another, its ears; the third, its tail; the fourth, its feet; and finally, the fifth, its penis. Everybody wanted to be the first to drink its milk. The one who grasped the donkey's penis called out that he could get milk there from. Then he began to extract. Finally, this group of people felt tired and bored, for they could not get what they had wanted. They got nothing in return, despite of their effort. They were all laughed at by the people at large.

This is also held to be true with the common heretics.

The heretics who learn their religious faith from some inadequate sources, might lead to illusions giving rise to all kinds of heterodox views such as to go naked, to fast, to jump into precipice or go through fire. With all these kinds of heterodox views, they fall to the evil paths, like those stupid men seeking in vain for milk from a male donkey.

Shredding Emotions and Desires

A veteran general, who was tired of wars, paid a special visit to Zen Master Dahui Zonggao and requested to be a Buddhist monk. He proposed: "Master! I have been disillusioned with the mortal world. Please show your mercy to take me in and allow me to be your disciple!"

Zen Master Zonggao replied: "You have a family and have already formed deep-rooted social habits. You are too worldly to be a Buddhist monk. Let's put this aside first."

The general insisted: "Master! I can let go of everything. My wife, my children or my family cannot keep me back from doing this. Please take the tonsure for me right away!"

Zen Master Zonggao said: "Not now, we will discuss it some other time."

There was nothing the general could do but left. The other day, he got up very early to pray to Buddha in the temple. Zen Master Zonggao saw and asked him: "Why did you come and pray to Buddha at such an early time?"

The general answered with a Buddhist hymn: "In order to

get rid of emotions and desires, I get up early to worship and pray to Buddha."

The Zen master cracked a joke on him with a Buddhist hymn as well: "You get up so early. Don't you worry that your wife would have a clandestine affair?"

The general felt offended by the remarks and cursed: "You old geezer! Your words are insulting!"

Zen Master Zonggao burst out laughing and said: "A slight fan can set fire to your emotions. With such a bad temper, how can you let go of everything?"

Everything Is Still There

A Zen monk Ikkyū had been meditating alone for quite a few days without uttering a word. His master saw him through and then brought him outside of the temple with a smile.

Outside the temple beautiful spring scenery was to be enjoyed – fresh air, peak green shoots of grass, birds darting through the air, and murmuring brooks.

Ikkyū took a deep breath and then peeked at his master. The master was composedly sitting at the hillside for Zen meditation.

A bit confused, Ikkyū had no idea of what the master was up to.

As the afternoon was passed, the master stood up and motioned Ikkyū back to the temple.

As soon as the master entered the door of the temple, he suddenly turned around and shut the double wood doors gently, leaving Ikkyū outside.

Not knowing what the master's intention, Ikkyū just sat outside alone to ponder on the master's motivation.

Very soon it got dark and the mist clouded the surrounding hills. The woods, the brooks, and the sound of birds and waves could be seen or heard no more.

At that moment, the master called Ikkyū from inside. Ikkyū opened the door and walked in.

The master asked, "How is everything outside?"

"It is all dark."

"Anything else?"

"Nothing at all."

"No," said the master, "Outside is fresh wind, green fields, flowers and plants, brooks ... everything is still there."

One and Two

In the history of Chinese Buddhism, Taoists and Buddhists often argued and competed with each other.

A Taoist said to Zen Master Fayin, "Your Buddhism will never be as good as our Taoism because the optimal situation of Buddhism is all about 'one mind', 'one method', 'one true dharma realm', 'one Buddha, one Tathagata'. All of these have only 'one' aspect. But everything in our Taoism has 'two' aspects. 'Two' is better than 'one', for example, our 'qian-kun', 'yin-yang' and etc.. All of these have 'two' aspects. To be honest, our 'two' is much better than your 'one'."

Zen Master Fayin then asked with doubt, "Really? Can your 'two' transcend 'one'?"

The Taoist said, "As long as you can come up with 'one' thing, I can make it 'two', so I can surely win."

Zen Master Fayin then lifted up one of his legs and crossed it to the other, saying unhurriedly, "Now I lift up one leg. Can you lift up two?"

The Taoist was left speechless.

One Word

A monk asked, "What is one word?"
Zen Master Joshu said, "Two words."

~ Case 257 of The Recorded Sayings of Zen Master Joshu

~

~ Translated by James Green ~

Weight

Once upon a time, a Korean Zen master, Kyong Ho, was traveling with his disciple, Man Gong, who had just become a Buddhist monk. The young disciple kept muttering about his heavy packs all the way and begged his master for a rest from time to time. But Zen Master Kyong Ho kept walking with a good spirit.

One day, while passing through a small village, they saw a woman leaving her house. Zen Master Kyong Ho, who was walking in front of his disciple, grabbed the woman's hand all of a sudden. The woman screamed and very soon her family and neighbors came to her help. They thought the master was sexually harassing the poor woman and started to chase after the two travelers, shouting and waving their fists. Zen Master Kyong Ho immediately turned around and fled desperately. The young disciple Man Gong ran like mad after his master, with packs on his back.

The two travelers kept running and running through trails and roads, until the villagers stopped chasing after them. The master suddenly stopped by a quiet pathway, turned around, and asked his disciple: "Still heavy now?"

"It's strange, Master. I don't even feel any heaviness of the packs while running."

The Jade Belt of Su Dongpo

One day, Zen Master Foyin was giving a lecture about Buddha Dharma in Jinshan Temple. The lecture hall was packed out when Su Dongpo finally arrived. Then Zen Master Foyin said: "It's all packed out. There's no seat for you."

Su Dongpo was always enthusiastic about Zen. Immediately, he replied wittily: "Well, since there's no seat for me, I would have to take your body of the four great elements and the five heaps as my seat."

Knowing that Su Dongpo was having a discussion of Zen with him, the Zen master answered, "Mr. Su, I have a question for you. If you can answer my question, then you can take my body as your seat. But if you can't, we will keep your jade belt as a souvenir here in the temple." Su Dongpo had always been a pompous man. He soon accepted the bet because he had full confidence in his victory. Then Zen Master Foyin asked: "The four great elements and the five heaps do not constitute any 'essence'. Where are you going to be seated?" Su Dongpo did not know how to respond.

Our material body is constituted by the four great elements, including solidity, fluidity, heat, and motion, none of which is tangible. Therefore, it is impossible to be seated on these intangible elements. As a result, Su Dongpo lost his jade belt to Zen Master Foyin. Up to the present, the belt still remains in Jinshan Temple.

The Abbot's Gift

A Zen monk, early in his training, is preparing to leave the monastery and switch locations, for that is common in the Zen practice. Before he leaves, he goes to the abbot of the monastery to say goodbye. He does so, but the abbot says he has a gift for him. Now, it is part of the Japanese way to accept gifts and be appreciative; to do otherwise is rude and, therefore, wrong. The abbot takes a pair of tongs and picks up a red-hot coal from the adjacent fire pit on which he has a tea kettle.

The young monk starts to contemplate what he should do, and after a few moments, runs out of the hall distressed, for he cannot figure out what he is supposed to do. He can take the coal and be burned, or he can refuse the gift of the abbot. Both, in his mind, are things he cannot do.

He meditates on the problem for the next week and comes back to say goodbye. However, the same scene is played again, and the same frustration is found when he tries to figure out what the abbot wants him to do.

He meditates further on the subject and feels he has discovered how to respond to the abbot's gift. He returns, for the third time, to say goodbye to the abbot, and as before the abbot picks up a red-hot coal and presents it as a gift to the young monk. The young monk simply replies, "Thank you."

The abbot breaks a grin, nods his head, and returns the coal to the fire pit. "You may go now," he says.

Buddha's Truth

During the Japanese occupation, a newly appointed governor-general named Minami came with a small retinue to have an audience with Master hyewol; his fame as the sage who had attained the state of no-mind had spread across Korea. After paying proper respect, the governor-general asked him, "Please tell me the most profound and loftiest truth of the Buddha."

Master Hyewol replied: "Buddha's truth? The loftiest and most profound truth? Hairs grow out of a ghost's fart."

Ghosts are already without substance, yet he was saying that these ethereal beings were farting; furthermore, hairs were growing from their farts. What in the world was he talking about? It was something that not only the governor-general couldn't comprehend, but even someone more advanced would have no way of understanding. The governor-general just sat there, unable to say a word, and then left. A rumor that Master Hyewol had hit the governor-general with a club quickly spread, even reaching Japan. One Japanese samurai, a student of Governor-general Minami, heard the story and vowed to himself, "I will go to Korea and teach that Korean monk Hyewol a hard lesson." When he arrived at the master's temple, without even removing his shoes he barged into the master's room brandishing a long samurai sword. Master hyewol was sitting on a cushion when the samurai put his naked sword to the master's neck. You must understand that this was a time when the Japanese did not consider Koreans as equals with the same human rights.

However, Master Hyewol maintained his composure and calmly pointed behind the samurai. A guilty conscience needs no accuser. Since he was about to commit the cowardly act of killing an innocent Seon master, he was afraid that somebody was going to attack him from behind. He spun around quickly, and at that moment Master Hyewol jumped up and slapped him on the back shouting, "Take my sword!"

The master's lightning-fast response startled the samurai. In awe of the master's ability, he sheathed his sword and prostrated himself in front of the master, saying, "A great master indeed." Then he left.

~ Finding the true self: Talks of the Seon Mountain Monk

~

~ Jinje Beopwon: Supreme Patriarch, Jogye Order of Korean Buddhism ~

Seoam Honggeun

Seoam Sunim died at Bongamsa on the 29th of March, 2003, at the age of 87. He had been a monk for sixty-eight years. Before his decease, he assembled about 100 monks and lay people from Taego Seon center and Bongam Monastery and told them, "I have nothing say. If people ask about my Nirvana poem, tell them, 'There was an old man who lived thus and died thus.' That is my Nirvana poem." He then retired to his room and passed away in a sitting position.

The Strange Teaching

Someone asked, "If people ask, 'What is the teaching of Joshu?,' what should I say?"

Zen master Joshu said, "Salt is expensive, rice is cheap."

NOTE: In ancient China, salt, being a monopoly of the state, was one of the most expensive commodities. The point of Joshu's answer lies in stating the commonplace.

~ Case 206 of Hoffman's Radical Zen ~

Buddha

Someone asked, "What is Buddha?"
Zen Master Joshu said, "Are you Buddha?"

~ Case 207 of Hoffman's Radical Zen ~

Yuanwu's "Gate of Misfortune"

A monk asked Yuanwu Keqin, "What is buddha?"
Yuanwu replied, "The mouth is the gate of misfortune."

~ Case 73 of Entangling Vines ~

Zen Master Xu Yun's Enlightenment

Xu-yun arrived at the Kao-min Ssu in 1895 to take part in meditation weeks, but since he had fallen in the river on the way, he was gravely ill. "Awaiting death," he says, " I sat firmly in the meditation hall day and night with increasing zeal." He continues:

" In the pure single-mindedness of my meditation, I forgot all about my body and twenty days later, my illness vanished completely. When the Abbot came with an offering of garments for the assembly, he was reassured and delighted to see that my appearance was radiant. He then spoke of my fall into the water and all the monks held me in great esteem. I was thus spared the trouble of working in the hall and could continue my meditation.

Henceforth, with all my thoughts brought to an abrupt halt, my practice took effect throughout day and night. My steps were as swift as if I were flying in the air. One evening after the set meditation period, I opened my eyes and suddenly perceived a great brightness similar to broad daylight wherein everything inside and outside the monastery was discernible to me. Through the wall, I saw the monk in charge of lamps and incense urinating outside, the guest-monk in the latrine, and far away, boats plying on the river with the trees on both its banks - all were clearly seen; it was just the third watch of the night when this happened. The next morning, I asked the incense-monk and guest-monk about this and both confirmed what I had seen the previous night. Knowing that this experience was only a temporary state I had attained, I did not pay undue regard to its strangeness. In the twelfth month during the third night of the eighth week set for training, an attendant came to fill our cups with tea after the meditation session ended. The boiling liquid accidentally splashed over my hand and I dropped the cup which fell to the ground and shattered with a loud report; instantaneously I cut off my last doubt about the Mind-root and rejoiced at the realization of my cherished aim. I then thought of the time when I left home, and of the time during which I had lived a wanderer's life, my illness in the hut on the banks of the Yellow River...

If I had not fallen into the water and been gravely ill, and if I had not remained indifferent to both favorable and adverse situations, I would have passed another life aimlessly and this experience would not have happened today. I then chanted the following gatha:

A cup fell to the ground
With a sound clearly heard.
As space was pulverized
The mad mind came to a stop."

~ Empty Cloud: The Autobiography of Chinese Zen
Master Xu Yun ~

Baizhang's New Paddy

Baizhang Weizheng (Niepan) of Hongzhao said to the monks, "If you clear a new rice paddy for me, I will explain to you the Great Principle."

After clearing the new paddy, the monks returned and asked the master to explain the Great Principle. The master held out his two hands.

~ Case 93 of Entangling Vines ~

What Time Is It Now?

In the early days of constructing Lin Quan Chan Monastery, the Grand Master Wei Chueh often led his disciples in "working meditation" by laboring at the construction site until past midnight. One night, a monk queried of the Master, "Master, it is already late. Is it time to take a break?" The Master asked, "What time is it now?" "It is one hour before midnight." The Master turned to him and said, "Oh! It is now just daytime in America."

The monk paused for a while and then continued to complete the work with the Master until one o'clock in the morning. When they were finished for the night, he realized that he did not feel sleepy at all. Suddenly, he realized the truth of the Master's words, "Sleeping is also a delusion."

The Way

A long time ago, a monk asked Zen Master Guizong [Zhichang], "What is the way?"

Guizong answered, "You are it."

Also, a monk asked Mazu [Guizong's teacher], "What is the way?"

Mazu said, "Ordinary mind is the way."

Also, there was a monk who asked an [unknown] ancient worthy, "What is the way?"

The person said, "What you have been going through is it."

Are these three venerable masters' sayings ultimately the same or different? If you say they are the same, ten are just five pairs. If you say they are different, eight ounces are half a pound. Ha!

~ Eihei Koroku ~
~ Zen Master Dogen ~

The Strange Verse

Zen Master Zihu Lizong (800-880) had a verse which he read to the assembly,
    Having lived thirty years in Zihu
    Getting energy on rice and vegetables twice a day
    Every day ascending the mountain a few times –
    Do you people of the present understand, or not?

Shuzan's Staff

SHUZAN held up his staff and waved it before his monks. "If you call this a staff," he said, "you deny its eternal life. If you do not call this a staff, you deny its present fact. Tell me just what do you propose to call it?"

Forms

BUTSUGEN said to his disciples; "Each of you has a pair of ears, but what have you ever heard with them? Each of you has a mouth, but what have you ever said with it? Each of you has eyes, but what have you ever seen with them? No, no! You have never heard, never spoken, never seen, never smelled.

"But in such a case where do all these colors, shapes, sounds, smells, come from?"

Zen

MATAJURA wanted to become a great swordsman, but his father said he wasn't quick enough and could never learn. So Matajura went to the famous dueller Banzo and asked to become his pupil. "How long will it take me to become a master?" he asked. "Suppose I became your servant, to be with you every minute; how long?"

"Ten years," said Banzo.

"My father is getting old. Before ten years have passed, I will have to return home to take care of him. Suppose I work twice as hard; how long will it take me?"

"Thirty years," said Banzo.

"How is that?" asked Matajura. "First you say ten years. Then when I offer to work twice as hard, you say it will take three times as long. Let me make myself clear: I will work unceasingly: no hardship will be too much. How long will it take?"

"Seventy years" said Banzo. "A pupil in such a hurry learns slowly."

Matajura understood. Without asking for any promises in terms of time, he became Banzo's servant. He cleaned, he cooked, he washed, he gardened. He was ordered never to speak of fencing or to touch a sword. He was very sad at this; but he had given his promise to the master and resolved to keep his word. Three years passed for Matajura as a servant.

One day while he was gardening, Banzo came up quietly behind him and gave him a terrible whack with a wooden sword. The next day in the kitchen the same blow fell again. Thereafter, day in, day out, from every corner and at any moment, he was attacked by Banzo's wooden sword. He learned to live on the balls of his feet, ready to dodge at any movement. He became a body with no desires, no thoughts - only eternal readiness and quickness.

Banzo smiled and started lessons. Soon Matajura was the greatest swordsman in Japan.

Void

Says the Master to his pupil: "Do you understand that you don't really exist?"

Upon which the pupil replies: "To whom are you telling that?"

Shadow

There was once a man who was terrified of his own shadow and lived in fear of the sound of his own footsteps. Walking along one day he entered a panic and tried to flee at top speed. But as fast as he ran, his shadow and footsteps kept up with him and made him run all the faster, until he finally collapsed of exhaustion and died.

If he had only sat down in the shade of a tree, he would no longer have have been able to see his shadow or hear his own footsteps.

The Two Goat-herders

Once upon a time in ancient China there were two men, Zang and Gu. Both were goat-herders. Zang liked to spend his time gambling with his friends. He often gambled while he was tending the goats. Gu was very serious about acquiring learning. He often read and studied while he tended his goats.

One day, Zang became very involved in his gambling, and one of his goats strayed and was lost.

That same day, Gu became very absorbed in a book he was studying in order to cultivate and improve himself. One of his goats strayed and was lost also.

~ Chuang Tzu ~

The Tiger in The City

A sage was dining as guest of the district magistrate. "Sir," said the sage. "Suppose you were eating your dinner and a man rushed up and told you that there was a tiger in the middle of the city. Would you believe him?"

"Just one man?"

"Just one."

"No, I wouldn't believe there was a tiger in the city if I only heard it from one man."

"What about two men?"

"Just two?"

"Just two."

The magistrate took longer to answer this time. Finally he said, "No, no, I don't think so. I wouldn't believe it if I only heard it from two men."

"What about three?"

"Yes," said the magistrate. "If I heard it from three men, I'd believe it."

"That's interesting," said the sage, "because there's still no tiger in the city."

~ Chinese Fable ~

Living On Opinion

Once when Lieh Tzu lived in Cheng he was very poor, and had trouble feeding his family. Unknown to him, a neighbor went to the prime minister and told him all about Lieh Tzu. "Look," the neighbor said. "This man is a true sage. It's shameful for the state to let he and his family starve. Wouldn't it be better for you to show that you can recognize and appreciate a true sage when you see one?"

The prime minister, impressed by the words of the neighbor, sent a servant to Lieh Tzu's home with a rich gift of money. But Lieh Tzu politely refused the gift.

After the servant left, Lieh Tzu's wife criticized him angrily. "You took food out of the mouths of your family!" she said. "It wouldn't have hurt to accept the gift!"

"If we live by someone's opinion, we can die by someone's opinion," said Lieh Tzu.

Shortly thereafter, the prime minister lost power and was executed, and all those he had favored came under suspicion.

~ Lieh Tzu ~

The Mosquito and The Carpenter

The Buddha, in one story, walks by a village and notices a carpenter with his son. A mosquito lands on the bald head of the carpenter, who asks his son to get it off. The son searches for something to swat it with it (apparently forgetting he has hands). The closest thing to the pair is an axe. The son grabs it and swings at his father's head, killing him on the spot.

The Buddha, later told his disciples: "A Senseless Friend Is Worse Than An Enemy."

How the Wicked Sons Were Duped

A very wealthy old man, imagining that he was on the point of death, sent for his sons and divided his property among them. However, he did not die for several years afterwards; and miserable years many of them were. Besides the weariness of old age, the old fellow had to bear with much abuse and cruelty from his sons. Wretched, selfish ingrates! Previously they vied with one another in trying to please their father, hoping thus to receive more money, but now they had received their patrimony, they cared not how soon he left them—nay, the sooner the better, because he was only a needless trouble and expense. And they let the poor old man know what they felt.

One day he met a friend and related to him all his troubles. The friend sympathised very much with him, and promised to think over the matter, and call in a little while and tell him what to do. He did so; in a few days he visited the old man and put down four bags full of stones and gravel before him.

"Look here, friend," said he. "Your sons will get to know of my coming here to-day, and will inquire about it. You must pretend that I came to discharge a long-standing debt with you, and that you are several thousands of rupees richer than you thought you were. Keep these bags in your own hands, and on no account let your sons get to them as long as you are alive. You will soon find them change their conduct towards you. Salaam. I will come again soon to see how you are getting on."

When the young men got to hear of this further increase of wealth, they began to be more attentive and pleasing to their father than ever before. And thus, they continued to the day of the old man's demise, when the bags were greedily opened, and found to contain only stones and gravel!

Blowing Out A Candle

The student came to the master one night and asked many questions. He was as full of questions as a melon is full of seeds. He kept asking them, one right after another, until late into the evening. It seemed that whenever the master answered one question there was another one waiting right behind it. The master could see that the student was trying to use his mind to understand dharma, which would get him nowhere.

Finally, the student seemed to notice the late hour and got to his feet, apologizing to the master for keeping him so late. He went to the door of the master's room and looked out at the dark night. 'It is very dark out there,' he said, a little nervous at venturing out into the gloom.

The master rose and offered a lit candle to the student, who took it gratefully. But before he had gone out of the door the master quickly bent over and blew the candle out. The student stood for a moment, watching the wisps of smoke floating above the blackened wick of the candle. In that moment his mind was opened, and he began to understand that all his questions had no purpose: that he himself was the true question and by the act of blowing out the candle the master had illuminated his mind. He found he had no more questions that day, or any other after it, and was content to sit quietly and watch the world flow by like the flickering flame of a candle.

Staying in the woods and living on herbs

Zen Master Tongda went into the Great White Mountains. He had no supply of grain, so when he was hungry, he ate herbs. He rested under the trees. He sat upright contemplating the mystery for five years without stopping. Once he happened to hit a clump of dirt with a stick, and when the clump of dirt broke up, he opened up in great enlightenment.

Wisdom Eye

The student came to the master and told him that the spring from which their community received their water had been plugged up by sand.

He bowed and waited to receive his orders. The master said nothing. The student bowed once more and turned to leave the room. Suddenly the master said, 'If the spring is obstructed by sand, what is your wisdom eye obstructed by?'

The student did not know what to say. He only worked in the grounds and, unlike the other students, never sat in meditation – nor could he read the sacred texts. He waited to hear the answer, hoping he would understand it when it came.

'Your wisdom eye', said the master, 'is obstructed by your eye.'

At this the student turned to go, shaking his head. When he heard a chuckle behind him he turned towards the master, who gave him a wide smile and nodded to him. At this the student's wisdom eye opened all at once and he fell to his knees in gratitude.

How to Speak?

The student went to ask the master some questions about the path of Zen but before he could get a word out, the master told him not to speak.

'Why can't I speak?' asked the student.

The master replied, 'First, close your mouth. Only then will you be able to speak.'

Outhouse Zen

A student of Zen had practised meditation for many years, hoping for the flash of insight termed satori. Yet, for all his discipline and years of strict meditation, he felt he was getting nowhere. His teacher was no help, repeatedly admonishing the student not to be attached to such experiences. But, one by one, all the other students reached, if not enlightenment, as least some level of true insight.

Finally, angry and frustrated, the student left the temple and went back to the 'world of dust'. On one of his first days there he visited an inn and had a big meal of meat and wine, both of which he had not touched during all his years in the temple.

Later, upon entering the privy and having squatted down to do his business, the sudden plop of his stool falling into the hole below awakened him in one moment to the clear insight he had been working towards for so many years!

Leaking Roof

As the roof was leaking, a Zen Master told two monks to bring something to catch the water. One brought a tub, the other a basket. The first was severely reprimanded, the second highly praised.

Tit Tit

A Zen Master was dying and the disciples had gathered. And his whole life he had been talking about here now – that's what Masters have been doing down through the ages. The disciples asked again, "Master, you are leaving us and we will be left in darkness. Is there any last message so that we can cherish it and remember it forever? We will keep it as a sacred memory in our hearts."

The Master opened his eyes... at that moment on the roof of his hut, a squirrel ran making noise –

TIT TIT, TEEVEE, TIT TIT – and the Master raised his hand and said, "THIS IS IT!" and died.

What is he saying, "This is it"? He is simply indicating. He is simply saying there is nothing to say – there is much to see, but there is nothing to say.

~ Osho: Walk Without Feet ~

The One Sword

Mind means duality and meditation, oneness. In Zen they call it – THE ONE SWORD.

Kusunoki Masashige came to a Zen monastery when he was about to meet the overwhelming army of Ashikaga Takanji and asked the Master: "When a man is at the parting of the ways between life and death how should he behave?"

The Master answered: "Cut off your dualism and let THE ONE SWORD stand serenely by itself against the sky!"

~ Osho: A Cup of Tea ~

Walk On

So never settle for anything. Always go on and on and on.

One Zen master, Rinzai, said to his master, "Now I have attained to enlightenment, what shall I do?"

The master said, "Walk on."

Walk on is the message.

So, whenever you feel that one peak is attained, feel happy, thankful, grateful – but remember that this is only a new challenge. Go on looking for a further and higher peak which must be hiding somewhere in the mist. Use every peak as a step to a further peak. If you go on growing, you remain on the peak.

~ Osho: Be Realistic, Plan for A Miracle ~

Posture

To stress the importance of assuming a proper posture when meditating, Shodo Harada told the story of "a rich man who wanted a third-floor residence so that he could be higher than any of his neighbours. When the carpenters arrived, they naturally began construction from the bottom floors. When the rich man saw this, he became angry and said to the carpenters, 'I said I wanted a third-floor residence, so I don't need anything else, just the third floor. Why should I waste my money building the bottom floors?'"

~ Shodo Harada – Cypress Trees in the Garden ~

Koan

When a monk asked Suzuki Shosan to assign him a koan, Shosan told him to keep his attention focused on the character for Death. No other koan, he said, was necessary. "Keep that alone in your heart and let all else go."

~ Suzuki Shosan – Zen Masters of Japan ~

Dogen with Chinese Master Rujing

All the monks were sitting in meditation in the meditation hall one early morning when the man next to Dogen dozed off — a common enough occurrence in early-morning sessions. But when Rujing came by on a routine inspection and saw the sleeping monk, he was for some reason particularly rankled.

Rujing roared: "Zazen means the dropping away of mind and body! What will you get by sleeping?"

Dogen, sitting nearby, was at first startled, but then an indescribable calm, an ecstatic joy washed over him.

Rujing immediately recognized his enlightenment to be genuine and he conferred upon Dogen the seal of patriarchal succession of his line of the Caodong sect. After two more years of study Dogen returned to Japan.

Beyond Words

Master I-tuan once said to his assembled monks, "To talk is blaspheming, to remain silent is deception. Beyond silence and talking there is an upward passage, but my mouth is not wide enought to point it out to you."

So, saying he left the hall.

~ The Spirit of Zen ~

Suspect

There was a man who lost his axe, and suspected the boy next door. He watched the boy walking: he had stolen the axe! His expression, his talk, his behaviour, his manner, everything about him betrayed that he had stolen the axe. Soon afterwards the man was digging in his garden and found the axe. On another day he saw the boy next door again; nothing in his behaviour and manner suggested that he would steal an axe.

~ The Book of Lieh Tzu ~

The Ultimate Secret

When Yün-men was asked for the ultimate secret of Zen, he replied, "Dumpling!"

~ The Way of Zen: Alan Watts ~

Gratitude

A man went to see a woman who was renowned for her wisdom, and asked her for advice. She told him, "Whatever happens to me, I always say, 'Thank you for everything. I have no complaints.'" The man went away but returned sometime later. "I have tried your advice, but do not feel any different," he told her. She replied, "Thank you for everything. I have no complaints." At this the man was enlightened.

~ The Zen Path Through Depression by Philip Martin ~

Kanzan's "Inherently Perfect Buddha"

The Sutra of Complete Enlightenment asks, "If we all are inherently perfect buddhas, why then have we become ignorant, deluded sentient beings?"

~ Case 175 of Entangling Vines ~

Don't Wait Until Next Life

A monk who had encountered an obstacle in his practice became doubtful as to whether or not he could complete the Path in this lifetime. He therefore asked the Master, "Shifu, in my next life..."

Before he could finish his question, the Master (Wei Chueh) immediately chided him, "Next life? In Zen practice, one maintains this present mind for an eon, and an eon exists in this present mind. In this very lifetime, liberate yourself from the cycle of life and death!"

Reasons

Lieh-tzu was studying archery and hit the target. He sought advice from Kuan-yin, who asked him: 'Do you know why you hit the target?'

'No.'

'It won't do yet. He went away to practice, and after three years again reported to Kuan-yin.

'Do you know why you hit the target?'

'I know.'

'It will do. Hold on to this knowledge and do not lose it.'

This applies, not only to archery, but to ruling the state and ruling oneself. Therefore, the sage scrutinises, not the fact of survival or ruin, but its reasons.

The Kitten and the Fly

A young student approached the master who was seated in the garden and asked "Master, no matter how hard I try I just can't achieve mindfulness."

The master said nothing but pointed to a corner of the garden where a kitten was attempting to capture a fly. The kitten lunged, gasped and stalked the fly. Yet for all of her efforts, the fly stayed just out of her reach.

Finally, the kitten wore herself out and curled up in a ball at the master's feet.

The fly, promptly landed, of its own accord, right on the tip of the sleeping kitten's nose.

The young student, seeing this, understood.

Hui-Neng

A monk told Hui-Neng (628-713, the Sixth Ancestor of Chinese Ch'an) about a poem by Chan Master Wo-lun which says:

Wo-lun has skill, he can cut off hundreds of thoughts.
When facing the outside states, his mind is not moved.
The Bodhi in his mind is growing day after day.

Hearing this Hui-neng said, "This poem does not concern the substance of the mind. If one practices according to it, one will become attached." Then he immediately recited this poem for the monk:

Hui-neng has no skill, he does not cut off hundreds of thoughts.
When facing the outside states, his mind moves often.
The bodhi is just this.

~ Yi Wu, The Mind of Chinese Ch'an ~

Why did Bodhidharma come from the west?

This is one of the most classical question in Zen. It means what is the ultimate truth, what is the actual teaching of Bodhidharma, or what is the meaning of life. Zen Master reply to this question in different unique manner.

When Zen Master Baiyun was asked this question, he said, "Birds fly, rabbits jump."

To Taste Apples

Once upon a time, there was an elderly man who sent a servant to buy him some apples. He gave him orders as follows, "You'll buy some good and sweet apples for me."

The servant then went on an errand with money. The owner of the apple orchard said to him, "All my apples are good and sweet: There is not a single bad one. You'll know it when you taste one."

The servant said, "I'll buy some after I taste every single one of them. How do I know about the rest, if I only taste one?"

After tasting them one by one, he bought the apples. The master did not like the sight of all these half-eaten apples and he threw them all out.

This is also held to be true with the people at large.

Buddha

Someone asked, "What is Buddha?"
Joshu said, "What are you? "

~ Case 376 of Radical Zen ~

The Master's Smile

A monk joyously approached the Master Wei Chueh in his office to report his meditation experience. The Master looked at him, smiled, and did not say anything. After a few days, this monk was annoyed by something, so he came again to the Master to complain about his difficulty. The Master still looked at him and smiled without saying a word.

Looking at the Master's familiar smile, this monk thought about the distinctly different state of mind that he was in a few days ago. The Master's smile reminded him of the Buddha's teaching, "To be calm in quietness is not true stillness; to be calm in chaos is true stillness."

Addressing

There is a famous story of a Zen master. Every day, waking up in the morning, he would shout his own name. His disciples were very much puzzled. Finally, they gathered courage and asked him.

The master said," Because only I am, there is nobody else to be called for. So, I declare as I wake up, 'Aha! So, I am here again!'"

~ Osho: From Death to Deathlessness ~

The Last Words

One story is told about the death of Zen master Roshi Taji: When Roshi Taji was close to death, a disciple brought him a cake. As Roshi Taji ate, he began to look worse. His disciples asked for his final words. His response: "My, but this cake is delicious!" Even in the face of

imminent death, he lived each moment fully. His last words, rather than being an attempt to utter some profundity, were an expression of his being completely present to the experience of tasting. The ephemeral nature of life, when completely embraced, heightens our experience.

~ Death, Dying, and the Afterlife: Lessons from World Cultures ~
~ Professor Mark Berkson, Hamline University ~

Life and Death

Someone said, "Life and death is here. How am I to cope with it?"

Master Ummen said, "Where is it?"

~ From Zen Miracles ~

The Last Instruction

On the day of his death, Kanzan Egen told his disciples, "I ask only this of you. Dedicate yourselves to the Great Matter!" Then he donned his travel clothes and went to stand quietly by a pond near the monastery's front gate. In this manner, he died.

~ Zen Masters of Japan ~

A Single Hair

Koun Ejo had practiced with Dogen for many years. At one point, Dogen brought up the expression, "A single hair pierces many holes."

Hearing this, Ejo was awakened. That evening he made bows to Dogen and asked: "Irrespective of the single hair, what are the many holes?"

Dogen smiled, saying, "Completely pierced."

Never loosening the belt of the garment

Zen teacher Zhao of Golden Light Temple left home when he was thirteen. At nineteen he went to Hongyang Mountain and took refuge with Master Jiaye. He served him diligently for three years. He never loosened the belt of his garment, and when he slept, he never lay down. He was still conducting himself like this when he opened up and was enlightened at Mount Gushe.

Think of Not-Thinking

One day after Yaoshan Weiyan had been seated in meditation for a long while, a monk asked him what he did during zazen: "What is it that you think of while you sit there as still as a mountain?"

"I think of not-thinking," Weiyen replied.

"How can you think of not-thinking?" the bewildered monk persisted.

"It isn't thought."

~ Zen Masters of China ~

Reward

There was a vagabond of Sung who offered to perform a trick before Lord Yuan. Lord Yuan summoned him and let him show what he could do. The man's trick was to fasten to his legs a pair of stilts twice as long as himself and run backwards and forwards juggling seven swords which he threw up in rotation, keeping five in the air at the same time. Lord Yuan was astounded, and at once gave him a present of gold and silk. There was another vagabond who could perform acrobatic tricks. Hearing of it, he too presented himself to Lord Yuan. Lord Yuan was furious, saying: Not long ago there was a man who came to me with an extraordinary trick. There was no point in the trick, but just then I happened to be in a good mood, so I gave him a present of gold and silk. This other man must have come because he heard about it and hopes for a reward from me too.' He had him bound and punished and did not loose him for a month.

~ The Book of Lieh Tzu ~

Ask Well

Another day a monk bowed.
Joshu said, "Ask well, ask well."
The monk asked, "What is Zen?"
Joshu said, "Today it is cloudy, so I will not answer."
NOTE: In "Today it is cloudy" Joshu is responsive to the moment. In the combination of "Today it is cloudy" and "so I will not answer" there is "nonsense" to parallel the nonsense of the monk's question.

~ Case 398 of Radical Zen ~

Land of Buddha

A monk is on a quest to find the land of Buddha. His search has taken years but finally he is near the land where Buddha lives. First, he needs to cross a river. As he is crossing the river, he sees a dead body float by. It is his own body. The monk gets a terrible shock and is stricken by grief. There he floats, dead. All he once was, all he once knew, floats downstream with the dark river. It is the first moment of his liberation.

~ ZEN: Stories from the east ~
~ Marc Brookhuis ~

Reflection

Li Bai (701-762), Chinese poet, considered one of China's Greatest men of letters.

A lover of beauty and wine, Li Bai met his death appropriately. According to popular tradition, he was out in a boat one evening. Trying to embrace the reflection of the moon, which shone full on the water, he fell in and drowned.

Smile

I lent a book of Zen stories once to a friend of mine, years and years ago, and he was in [the] hospital. And when he gave it back to me, he said, 'Geez, I didn't understand a word of it, but it cheered me up enormously.'

~ Alan Watts ~

A Pound of Butter

Once, there was a farmer who regularly sold butter to a baker. One day, the baker decided to weigh the butter to see if he was getting the exact amount that he asked for. He found out that he wasn't, so he took the farmer to court.

The judge asked the farmer if he uses any measure to weigh the butter. The farmer replied, "Your Honor, I'm primitive. I don't have a proper measure, but I do have a scale."

The judge replied, "Then how do you weight the butter?"

The farmer replied, "Your Honour, long before the baker started buying butter from me, I have been buying a pound loaf of bread from him. Every day, when the baker brings the bread, I put it on the scale and give him the same weight in butter. If anyone is to be blamed, it's the baker."

Moral of the story: In life, you get what you give. Don't try to cheat others.

The Old Man and the Tea

In ancient China, a monk was speaking about the lack of serious students. A small group that followed him felt saddened, having believed that they were all worthy protégé's of the elderly teacher, who was already over 100 years old.

"Teacher, why do you speak so? We are your students, and have already learned much from you."

The old man retorted, "I am speaking of real knowledge and preparedness. I seek students who are ready to embark on the way of enlightenment. You are not yet ready."

One of the young followers replied, "Please tell us how to prepare. What must we do?"

At that, the old man smiled and said, "Whosoever knows how to do just one thing well, even if it is to prepare a simple cup of tea, with full attention, that person is wise enough to begin."

Everything is Beautiful

The disciple, visiting the master, exclaimed, "Wow, wow, wow! This is a beautiful patch of land you live on!"

And the master, looking at the disciple, with a hint of a smile, responded saying, "When you have a beautiful mind everything, and everyone, and everywhere is beautiful."

Information

A priest offered a lift to a Nun. She got in and crossed her legs, forcing her gown to reveal a leg. The priest nearly had an accident. After controlling the car, he stealthily slid his hand up her leg. The nun said, "Father, remember Psalm 129?" The priest removed his hand. But, changing gears, he let his hand slide up her leg again. The nun once again said, "Father, remember Psalm 129?" The priest apologized "Sorry sister but the flesh is weak." Arriving at the convent, the nun went on her way. On his arrival at the church, the priest rushed to look up Psalm 129. It said, "Go forth and seek, further up, you will find glory."

Moral of the story: If you are not well informed in your job, you might miss a great opportunity.

Enlightenment in Seven Days

Buddha told his disciples: whoever makes an effort can attain enlightenment in seven days. If he can't manage it, certainly he will attain it in seven months, or in seven years. The young man decided that he would attain it in one week, and he wanted to know what he should do: "Meditation" was the reply.

The young man began to practice, but in ten minutes he was already distracted. Little by little, he began paying attention to everything that distracted him, and thought that he was not wasting time, but was getting used to himself.

One fine day he decided it was not necessary to arrive at his goal so fast, because the path was teaching him many things.

It was at that moment that he became an Enlightened one.

The Cynics

Antisthenes (445-365 BC)

Vote

He used to recommend the Athenians to vote that asses are horses. When they deemed this absurd, his reply was, "But yet generals are found among you who had had no training but were merely elected."

Praise

"Many men praise you," said one.

"Why, what wrong have I done?" was his rejoinder.

Religions

Antisthenes (445-365 BC) was a disciple of Socrates. Once he met a priest who bragged that religious initiates like himself would be rewarded splendidly in the afterlife. Antisthenes acidly replied, "Why don't you die, then?"

Diogenes Of Sinope (412-323 BC)

"Of what use is a philosopher who doesn't hurt anybody's feelings?"

~ Diogenes Of Sinope (412-323 BC) ~

Important Talk

When one day he was gravely discoursing and nobody attended to him, he began whistling, and as people clustered about him, he reproached them with coming in all seriousness to hear nonsense, but slowly and contemptuously when the theme was serious.

Philosophers

Being asked why people give to beggars but not to philosophers, he said, "Because they think they may one day be lame or blind, but never expect that they will turn to philosophy."

Laugh

When someone said, "Most people laugh at you," his reply was, "And so very likely do the asses at them; but as they don't care for the asses, so neither do I care for them."

Philosophy

One day observing a youth studying philosophy, he said, "Well done, Philosophy, that thou divertest admirers of bodily charms to the real beauty of the soul."

Persuasion

He was asking alms of a bad-tempered man, who said, "Yes, if you can persuade me." "If I could have persuaded you," said Diogenes, "I would have persuaded you to hang yourself."

Spit

Once Diogenes the Cynic (412-323 BC) was invited into a rich man's fabulous house. He looked around at the opulent furnishings, and then spat in the owner's face. He then explained to the shocked man that everything else in the house was too nice to spit on.

Religious Thieves

Once Diogenes the Cynic (412-323 BC) saw the officials of a temple leading away someone who had stolen a bowl belonging to the treasurers, and said, "The great thieves are leading away the little thief."

Offerings

Seeing offerings at another temple, left in thanks by people who had survived storms at sea, Diogenes the Cynic (412-323 BC) pointed out that there would be many more offerings if they'd instead been left by the ones who didn't survive.

Hunger

When Diogenes the Cynic (412-323 BC) was asked why he was eating in the middle of the marketplace, he said, "That's where I got hungry" Notoriously, he also gratified himself sexually in public, and when challenged, replied with the immortal line, "I only wish I could get rid of hunger by rubbing my belly"

Crates of Thebes (365-285 BC)

He was a Cynic philosopher. Crates gave away his money to live a life of poverty on the streets of Athens. But Crates' toughness didn't prevent him from finding love—in a relationship much celebrated in the ancient literature, a well-born woman named Hipparchia (350-280 BC) married him and joined in the Cynic lifestyle. Her brother Metrocles also joined the Cynic cause. It is reported that Crates and Hipparchia followed Diogenes' example of public self-pleasuring by having sex right out in the open.

If you're thinking that the debauched Greeks wouldn't have been shocked by this, think again: they were shocked. And that was the point.

It is said that Crates is supposed to have initiated his son into sex by taking him to a brothel, and he allowed his daughter a month's trial marriage to potential suitors.

<u>Again</u>

When Alexander inquired whether he would like his native city to be rebuilt, his answer was, "Why should it be? Perhaps another Alexander will destroy it again."

Realization

There was a Zen student under a Master to whom he was very much devoted. Each time he approached the Master, the latter waved his hand, saying, "Not yet, not yet." Some time passed.

One evening he became desperate: "How can this be? I have no word of instruction which will lead me to the realization. The Master simply chases me, saying, 'Not yet, not yet.' What can I do? What do I have to think about it all?"

He went on like this – thinking, brooding, meditating – in utter desperation, but tenaciously clinging to his object of inquiry and pondering it from every possible point of view, when all of a sudden something flashed on his mind and he realized at once what the Master wanted him to discover.

The following morning, he visited the Master, wishing to let him know what happened to him. But the Master seeing him come burst out, "You have it now, you have it now!"

~ Osho: Ecstasy, The Forgotten Language ~

Preparation

There is a story of three woodcutters. The first immediately started chopping the tree. The second sharpened his axe for a short time and then began to chop. The third spent a lot of time sharpening the axe.

In the beginning, the first two woodcutters laughed at the third. But then he started chopping and by lunch he had finished the job. He went home carrying his load. Now he was the one laughing.

Spend time sharpening the axe. Sit over the sharpening stone and rub the blade against it. Hone and hone. When you're ready, go to cut, your effort won't be wasted. You won't need to use much force. You can work quickly and cleanly. The blade will do the work.

~ Chan Master Guo Jun ~
~ Essential Chan Buddhism ~

The Way

"What is seeing into the Way?" asked a monk.

Zen Master Xiangyan turned his fan around and said, "See this?"

The monk had no reply.

The Deepest Principle

Someone asked Zen Master Lingshu Rumin of Shaozhou, "What is the deepest principle of Zen?"
The master merely opened his hands.

Outside

A monk asked, "What is a person who is outside the three worlds?"

Zen Master Joshu said, "But I am inside the three worlds."

~ Case 406 of The Recorded Sayings of Zen Master Joshu
~
~ Translated by James Green ~

Same or Different?

A monk asked Zen Master Baiyun Shixing, 'The purport of the teachings and the purport of the patriarchs, are these two the same or different?'

'Not different.'

'Then they are the same.'

'Do not become obstructed by clever words,' said the master.

The Principal Thrust

A monk asked Zen Master Hengzhou Guangfan, 'What is the principal thrust of the Buddha-dharma (way of awakening)?'

'Verification,' replied the master.

Sweet

Mulla Nasrudin, in the Sufi tradition, was sitting, eating hot peppers, and crying because each one was bitter. Then he ate the next one and it was more bitter, then the next one. He hated it.

They said to him, "Why are you eating all these hot peppers?"

He said, "I'm waiting for a sweet one."

That's like us, waiting for a sweet one—a sweet sitting, a person, a situation.

~ Zen Miracles ~

Tao

A monk asked Zen Master Fayan Wenyi, 'In search for the Buddha's wisdom and insight, which road is the most direct?' 'Nothing better than this,' answered the master.

The Meaning

A monk asked, 'A hundred years in a dark room can be dispelled by a single light – what does this mean?'

Zen master Zhangyi Daoqin replied, 'Do not use such insulting language!'

The Essence

'What is the essence of the profound?'

'It does not come out of your mouth,' replied the master Touzi Datong.

Same or Different?

A monk asked Zen Master Lepu Yuan'an, 'The meaning of the patriarchs and that of the teachings – are these one or are they two?'

'In the lion's den there are no other beasts. The tracks of elephants contain no traces of fox prints,' said the master.

Kill the Buddha

Chikamasa was a pupil of the well-known master Ikkyu Sojun (1394-1481). According to folklore, Chikamasa was greeted at the hour of his death by the three Buddhas of the past, the present, and the future, riding on purple clouds with twenty-five escorts. Chikamasa first ordered his son to bring him his weapons, then shot an arrow at the Buddha in the center. The warrior thus showed his contempt for the celestial retinue and his unconcern for the world to come. Before his death, Chikamasa said this poem:

Umarenuru
sono akatsuki ni
shininureba
kyō no yūbe wa
akikaze zo fuku

Meaning:
One day you are born
you die the next—
today,

at twilight,
autumn breezes blow.

~ Book: Japanese Death Poems ~
~ Yoel Hoffmann ~

The Question

Daigu (d. 1669) was raised in a Zen monastery. While he was still a young monk, a woman asked him to hold a funeral service for her son. After the burial she asked, "Where has my child gone?" Daigu had no answer for her, and the incident shook him profoundly. He abandoned the monastery and went to be alone in the mountains.

~ Book: Japanese Death Poems ~
~ Yoel Hoffmann ~

Three Scholars

Once three scholars on the way to the civil service examination stopped to buy refreshments from a woman who sold pastries by the wayside. One man was calm and quiet, while the other two argued over literature. The woman asked where they were going. The latter two told her they were going to take the civil service examination. She said, "You two scholars won't pass the exam; that other man will." The two men swore at her and left.

When the results of the examination turned out as the woman had predicted, the two scholars who had failed went back to find out how she had known they would not pass, while the third man would. They asked her if she knew physiognomy. "No," she said, "all I know is that when a pastry is thoroughly cooked, it sits there quietly, but before it's finished it keeps on making noise."

~ Wu-men ~
~ Book: Classics of Buddhism and Zen, Volume 2, tr.
Thomas Cleary ~

The Strange Book

The Meditator Chen Jianmin (1906-1987) has written a book called "The Lighthouse in the Ocean of Chan". This is the opening talk of that book:

"Who told you to open this book? What are you lacking of? You should be given thirty blows even before opening it. If you have taken it up on yourself already, and throw up upon encountering it, then you would be spared the shout that would deafen you for three months. Even though mentioning the koans, understand the sentence after Nirvana, the ultimate matter is still not there. Thirty blows, receive them yourself."

Transmission

A Master, knowing his death was close, wanted to choose a successor among his senior students to transmit the teaching. He called three of them, drew three dots in the sand and asked each student what they see.

The first one said: "I see a triangle."

The second one exclaimed: "I see a house."

The third one stated: "I see three dots in the sand." He received the transmission.

Dilemma

There was a master walking in the forest with a group of his disciples, and suddenly he picked up a tree branch and said to one of the monks, "What is it?" And the monk hesitated; didn't answer immediately, so the teacher hit him with it. So, he turned to another monk and said, "What is it?" And the monk said, "Give it to me, so that I can see." And the master tossed him the branch. He caught it and he hit the master with it. And so, the master said, "Well, you got out of that dilemma."

~ Alan Watts ~

The Impermanence of Life

The Buddha asked a shramana, "How long can one be sure of staying alive?"

"A few days," was the reply.

The Buddha said, "You do not know about life."

He asked another shramana, "How long can one be sure of staying alive?"

"The length of a meal," was the reply.

The Buddha said, "You do not know about life."

He then asked another shramana, "How long can one be sure of staying alive?"

The reply was "A single breath."

The Buddha said, "Well said, you know about life!"

~ The Sutra of 42 Chapters, Chapter 38 ~

The Face

Question: 'Before mother and father were born, where was your face?'

'After you mother and father were born, where is your face?' replied the Zen master Nanquan Puyuan.

The Matter

A monk asked the Venerable Wansui of Zhengzhou (Henan, Zhengding), 'The great assembly is gathered like clouds – to discuss what?'

'The introduction to Chapter One,' replied the master.

The Essential Matter

'Please, may the master say something about the essential matter.'

Zen Master Xiufu Wukong replied, 'Take care!'

Secret

A little story about a Zen Master:

A disciple asked the Master, "What is Buddha's truth?"

The Master said, "Why not ask about your own mind or self instead of somebody else's?"

"What then is my self, O Master?" asked the disciple.

"You have to see what is known as 'the secret act.'"

"What is 'the secret act'? Tell me, Master," asked the disciple.

The Master opened his eyes and closed them.

This is the secret act.

~ Osho: Ecstasy, The Forgotten Language ~

Pricking oneself with an awl

Ciming [987-1040], Guquan, and Langye were comrades when they studied with Fenyang [947-1024]. At the time it was bitter cold in that region of China, Hedong, and it was causing the congregation much distress. Ciming's intent was set on the Path, and he never forgot it day or night. When he felt sleepy as he was sitting at night, he would take an awl and prick himself to stay awake. Later he became Fenyang's successor and greatly energized the wind of the Path. He was called the "Lion of West River".

The Teaching

A monk asked Chan master Daochang Runa, 'What is the meaning of the teachings?'

'To look for yourself,' replied the master.

The seven wonders of the world

A group of American school children were asked to list what they thought were the present "Seven Wonders of The World." Though there were some disagreements, the following received the most votes:

1. Egypt's Great Pyramids
2. Taj Mahal
3. Grand Canyon
4. Panama Canal
5. Empire State Building
6. St. Peter's Basilica
7. Great Wall of China

While gathering the votes, the teacher noted that one student had not finished her paper yet. So, she asked the girl if she was having trouble with her list. The little girl replied, "Yes, a little. I couldn't quite make up my mind because there are so many." The teacher said, "Well, tell us what you have, and maybe we can help." The girl hesitated, then read, "I think the "Seven Wonders of The World" are:

1. To see
2. To hear
3. To touch
4. To taste
5. To feel
6. To laugh
7. To love

The room was so quiet you could hear a pin drop. The things we overlook as simple and ordinary and that we take for granted are truly wondrous. A gentle reminder - that the most precious things in life cannot be built by hand or bought by man.

The Purpose

Someone asked, "What was the purpose of the [Patriarch's] coming from the West?"

Zen master Rinzai said, "If he had had a purpose, he couldn't have saved even himself."

The Buddha

A monk asked, 'What is Buddha?'

'Were I to tell you, it would be something apart,' said the Zen master Fashi Cezhen (905-979 CE).

The Meaning

A monk asked, "Why did Bodhidharma come from the west?"

Zen Master Fojian said, "If you taste vinegar, then you know sour. If you taste salt, then you know saltiness."

The Meaning

A monk asked Yangshan [Huiji], "What is the meaning of the Patriarch's coming from the West?" Yangshan drew a circle in the air with a finger and wrote a Chinese character of "Buddha" inside the circle. The monk was in silence.
(The Record of Transmission of the Lamp; Volume 11)

Why?

A monk asked, "Why did the First Ancestor come from the west?"

Zen Master Xingyan said, "I don't deal with that question."

Love Stays

A nurse took the tired, anxious serviceman to the bedside. "Your son is here," she said to the old man. She had to repeat the words several times before the patient's eyes opened. Heavily sedated because of the pain of his heart attack, he dimly saw the young uniformed marine standing outside the oxygen tent. He reached out his hand. The marine wrapped his toughened fingers around the old man's limp ones, squeezing a message of love and encouragement.

The nurse brought a chair so that the marine could sit beside the bed. All through the night, the young marine sat there in the poorly lighted ward, holding the old man's hand and offering him words of love and strength. Occasionally, the nurse suggested that the Marine move away and rest awhile. He refused. Whenever the nurse came into the ward, the marine was oblivious of her and of the night noises of the hospital – the clanking of the oxygen tank, the laughter of the night staff members exchanging greetings, the cries and moans of the other patients.

Now and then she heard him say a few gentle words. The dying man said nothing, only held tightly to his son all through the night. Along towards dawn, the old man died. The marine released the now lifeless hand he had been holding and went to tell the nurse. While she did what she had to do, he waited. Finally, she returned. She started to offer words of sympathy, but the Marine interrupted her.

"Who was that man?" he asked. The nurse was startled, "He was your father," she answered.

"No, he wasn't," the marine replied. "I never saw him before in my life."

"Then why didn't you say something when I took you to him?"

"I knew right away there had been a mistake, but I also knew he needed his son, and his son just wasn't here. When I realised that he was too sick to tell whether or not I was his son, knowing how much he needed me, I stayed."

The next time someone needs you ... just be there. Stay!

The Meaning

Daibai was asked by a monk, "What is the meaning of Bodhidharma coming from the west?"

Daibai replied, "His coming has no meaning!"

No Supernatural

One of my students brought a chi kung master renowned for what's called "third-eye vision" to my monastery. He carefully inspected me and told my student that there was light coming from my forehead, and it was very bright.

"Then why do I still need to turn on the light when I go into a dark room at night?" I asked.

Another chi kung master said I must have very high wisdom because he could see lots of little lotuses growing out of the top of my head.

[...]

IN CHINESE WE have a saying: "The blind cat caught a dead mouse." If you get caught up in such supernatural exploits, in the end you became a fool. The purpose of Chan is not to achieve supernatural or extrasensory power.

What if it is not only you but everyone in the room who experiences supernatural phenomena? On my meditation retreats, people often report a light shining from between the eyebrows of the statue of the Buddha on the altar of the Chan Hall where they meditate. They respectfully wish to know if the light is real.

"Treat it as if it is a dream, something illusionary," I say. "Reflect on the words of the Diamond Sutra: *'Fan so you siang cie se xi huan*. All phenomena are like a dream, illusionary, a mirage.' Return to your breath."

~ Chan Master Guo Jun ~
~ Essential Chan Buddhism ~

The Tao

Someone asked a Zen Master, "What is the Tao?"

"Do not try to nail a peg into empty space," repied the master.

The Stick

GOKU KYONEN
(*Died on the eighth day of the tenth month, 1272 at the age of fifty-six*)
The truth embodied in the Buddhas
Of the future, present, past;
The teaching we received from the
Fathers of our faith
Can all be found at the tip of my stick.

When Goku felt his death was near, he ordered all his monk-disciples to gather around him. He sat at the pulpit, raised his stick, gave the floor a single tap with it, and said the poem above. When he finished, he raised the stick again, tapped the floor once more and cried, "See! See!" Then, sitting upright, he died.

~ Book: Japanese Death Poems ~
~ Yoel Hoffmann ~

The Sage

In Japan the Zen people have a very beautiful saying. Somebody asked a Zen master, 'What is the definition of a sage?'

The master said, 'A sage is one who hopes that the rains will come after the summer and that winter will follow the rains.'

The man was puzzled, because this is how it happens, so what is the point of saying it? He said,

'Are you in your senses? What are you saying? –" A sage is a person who hopes that summer will be followed by rains and rains will be followed by winter"?'

The master said, 'I am talking in my senses. Yes, that's exactly what I mean.'

And the man said, 'That's how it happens!'

The master laughed and he said, 'The sage is one who always hopes only for that which already happens. He never hopes against it He simply hopes that two and two will be four, so of course, all his hopes are fulfilled. How can you frustrate a sage? – because he only hopes for that to which life is already moving.

~ Osho: God Is Not for Sale ~

Kindness

The good people of Han-tan were in the habit, every New Year's day, of presenting their Governor, Chien Tzu, with a number of live pigeons. This pleased the Governor very much, and he liberally rewarded the donors. To a stranger who asked the meaning of the custom, Chien Tzu explained that the release of living creatures on New Year's Day was the sign of a benevolent disposition. 'But,' rejoined the stranger, 'the people, being aware of your Excellency's whim, no doubt exert themselves to catch as many pigeons as possible, and large numbers must get killed in the process. If you really wish to let the birds live, the best way would be to prohibit the people from capturing them at all. If they have to be caught first in order to be released, the kindness does not compensate for the cruelty.' Chien Tzu acknowledged that he was right.

The Source

A monk asked Zen Master Zhiyong, 'What is the original source of all the Buddhas?'

'What is the source of this question?', replied the master.

Jewels Under the Saddle

Once upon a time, what happened did happen..... or you wouldn't be hearing this story!!

A merchant on a casual jaunt through a market, came across a fine specimen of a camel for sale.

The merchant and the camel seller, both skilled negotiators, struck a hard bargain. The camel seller pleased with his skill of worming out what he felt was a very good price, parted with his camel and the merchant chuffed that he had struck a fantastic bargain, proudly walked home with the latest addition to his large livestock.

On arriving home, the merchant called to his servant to come and help him take out the camel's saddle. The unwieldy heavily padded saddle being too difficult for the servant to manage on his own.

Hidden under the saddle, the servant found a small velvet pouch which on opening he discovered to be filled with precious jewels!!

The servant was overexcited!!! "Master you bought a camel.....but see what came FREE along with it!!!"

The merchant was astonished as he looked at the jewels

in his servants' palm. They were of extraordinary quality sparkling and twinkling in the sunlight.

"I bought the camel" he said, "not the jewels. I must return them to the camel seller immediately."

The servant was aghast.....his master was really foolish.

"Master.....no one will know."

But the merchant headed right back to the market and handed over the velvet pouch back to the camel seller.

The camel seller was very happy, " I had forgotten that I hid these jewels in the saddle for safe keeping."

"Here, choose one of the jewels for yourself, as a reward."

The merchant said, "I paid a fair price for the camel and the camel only, so NO thank you, I do not need any reward."

But as much as the merchant refused, the camel seller insisted.

Finally, the merchant said, sheepishly smiling, " Actually when I decided to bring the pouch back to you, I already took two of the most precious jewels and kept them for myself."

At this confession the camel seller was a bit flabbergasted and quickly emptied the pouch to count the jewels. However, he was very confused.

"All my jewels are here. What jewels did you keep?"

"The two most precious," said the camel seller.

"My INTEGRITY and my SELF RESPECT!"

Roger Jenkins explained it as "The ability to do the right thing or choosing to do the right thing when you could get away with doing the wrong thing."

The Meaning

Master Shoku was asked by a monk, "What is the meaning of our founder coming from the west?"

The master said, "It is like getting a man out of a thousand-foot-deep well without using one single inch of rope. This answers your enquiry."

The Meaning

Someone asked, "What did the Patriarch intend in coming from the West?"

Zen Master Yunmen replied, "That's as clear as day!"

The Meaning

A monk asked, "What is the meaning of Bodhidharma's coming from the West?"

Zen Master Joshu stood up.

The monk said, "So that's what it means."

Joshu said, "I haven't said anything yet."

The Meaning

A monk asked, 'What is the deep meaning of the Buddha's Dharma (the way of awakening)?'
Zen master Magu Baoche maintained silence.

The Meaning

Someone asked: "What is the meaning of Bodhidharma's coming from the West?"

Zen Master Ling-shu Jiu-min remained silent.

The Meaning

When Zen Master Hsueh-feng and his disciple, Hsuan-sha were repairing a fence, the latter put the question: "What is the meaning of Bodhidharma's coming from the West?".

Hsueh-feng merely shook the fence.

The Business

A monk asked, 'What is the business of our school?'
Zen Master Xuansha Shibei replied, 'Wait until your awakening, then it will come to you.'

The Essence

A small story:

A certain holy man accepted a pupil and said to him, "It would be a good thing if you tried to write down all you understand about the religious life and what has brought you to it."

The pupil went away and began to write. A year later he came back to the master and said, "I have worked very hard on this, and though it is far from complete, these are the main reasons for my struggle."

The master read the work, which was many thousands of words, and then said to the young man, "It is admirably reasoned and clearly stated, but it is somewhat long. Try to shorten it a little." So the novice went away and after five years he came back with a mere hundred pages.

The master smiled, and after he had read it he said, "Now you are truly approaching the heart of the matter. Your thoughts have clarity and strength. But it is still a little long; try to condense it, my son."

The novice went away sadly, for he had labored hard to

reach the essence. But after ten years he came back, and bowing low before the master offered him just five pages and said,

"This is the kernel of my faith, the core of my life, and I ask your blessings for having brought me to it."

The master read it slowly and carefully: "It is truly marvellous," he said, "in its simplicity and beauty, but it is not yet perfect. Try to reach a final clarification."

And when the master had reached the time appointed and was preparing for his end, his pupil returned to him again, and kneeling before him to receive his blessings handed him a single sheet of paper on which was written nothing.

Then the master placed his hands on the head of his friend and said, "Now... now you have understood."

~ Osho: The Heart Sutra ~

The Two Pebbles

Many years ago, in a small Italian town, a merchant had the misfortune of owing a large sum of money to the money-lender. The moneylender, who was old and ugly, fancied the merchant's beautiful daughter, so he proposed a bargain. He said he would forgo the merchant's debt if he could marry the daughter. Both the merchant and his daughter were horrified by the proposal.

The moneylender told them that he would put a black pebble and a white pebble into an empty bag. The girl would then have to pick one pebble from the bag. If she picked the black pebble, she would become the moneylender's wife and her father's debt would be forgiven. If she picked the white pebble, she need not marry him, and her father's debt would still be forgiven. But, if she refused to pick a pebble, her father would be thrown into jail.

They were standing on a pebble-strewn path in the merchant's garden. As they talked, the moneylender bent over to pick up two pebbles. As he picked them up, the sharp-eyed girl noticed that he had picked up two black pebbles and put them into the bag. He then asked the girl to pick her pebble from the bag.

The girl put her hand into the bag and drew out a pebble. Without looking at it, she fumbled and let it fall onto the pebble-strewn path where it immediately became lost among all the other pebbles. "Oh, how clumsy of me," she said. "But never mind, if you look into the bag for the one that is left, you will be able to tell which pebble I picked."

Sometimes it is necessary to think out of the box or, in this case, out of the bag.

Focus

In olden days Abbot Jimyo, sitting in meditation day and night through the bitter winter, found himself often invaded by the demon of sleep. He took a gimlet and drove it into his thigh with the words: "The light of the ancient sages was made great through piercing sufferings. Alive to achieve nothing, and to die unknown to any, what use is such a life?"

Mirror

Long ago Zen master Seppo asked: 'What if you suddenly come upon a mirror?' To which his disciple Gensha replied: 'Into a hundred fragments!' Smash it to pieces was his reply.

The Buddha

A monk asked Master Guxian Jin, 'What is Buddha?' 'Point to yourself,' said the master.

The Final Verse

As Kokan was nearing death, his foremost disciple asked him for a final verse. He hollered, "My final verse fills the universe! Why bother with pen and paper!"

The Ill Zen Master

A great Zen Master lay critically ill. As his doctor prepared to leave, he said cheerfully, "I will see you in the morning."

Although the dying Master knew his hours were numbered, he could not resist quipping, "Of course. But will I see you?"

~ Osho: I am That ~

The Rooster Prince

In a distant land, a prince lost his mind and imagined himself a rooster. He sought refuge under the table and lived there, naked, refusing to partake of the royal delicacies served in golden dishes – all he wanted and accepted was the grain reserved for the roosters. The king was desperate. He sent for the best physicians, the most famous specialists; all admitted their incompetence. So did the magicians. And the monks, the ascetics, the miracle-makers; all their interventions proved fruitless.

One day an unknown sage presented himself at court. "I think that I could heal the prince," he said shyly. "Will you allow me to try?"

The king consented, and to the surprise of all present, the sage removed his clothes, and joining the prince under the table, began to crow like a rooster.

Suspicious, the prince interrogated him: "Who are you and what are you doing here?" – "And you," replied the sage, "who are you and what are you doing here?" – "Can't you see? I am a rooster!" – "Hmm," said the Sage, "how very strange to meet you here!" – "Why strange?" – "You mean you don't see? Really not? You don't see that I am a rooster just like you?"

The two men became friends and swore never to leave each other.

And then the sage undertook to cure the prince by using himself as an example. He started by putting on a shirt. The prince couldn't believe his eyes. – "Are you crazy? Are you forgetting who you are? You really want to be a man?" – "You know," said the Sage in a gentle voice, "you mustn't ever believe that a rooster who dresses like a man ceases to be a rooster." The prince had to agree. The next day both dressed in a normal way. The sage sent for some dishes from the palace kitchen. "Wretch! What are you doing?" protested the prince, frightened in the extreme. "Are you going to eat like them now?" His friend allayed his fears: "Don't ever think that by eating like man, with man, at his table, a rooster ceases to be what he is; you mustn't ever believe that it is enough for a rooster to behave like a man to become human; you can do anything with man, in his world and even for him, and yet remain the rooster you are."

And the prince was convinced; he resumed his life as a prince.

~ Souls on Fire: Portraits and Legends of Hasidic Master
~
~ Elie Wiesel ~

Buddha in the Wallet

A ticket collector in a train found an old worn-out wallet in a compartment full of people. He looked inside to find the name of its owner. There was no clue. All that there was in it was some money and a picture of Buddha.

He held it up and asked, "Who does this wallet belong to?"

An old man said, "That's my wallet, Sir, please give it to me." The ticket collector said, "You'll have to prove that it is yours. Only then I can hand it over to you."

The old man, with a toothless smile, said. "It has a picture of Buddha in it." The ticket collector said, "That is no proof; anyone can have a picture of Buddha in his wallet. What is special about that? Why is your picture not there in it like most normal people?"

The old man took a deep breath and said, "Let me tell you why my picture is not there in it. My father gave this wallet to me when I was in school. I used to get a small sum as pocket money then. I had kept a picture of my parents in it. When I was a teenager I was greatly enamoured by my good looks. I removed my parent's picture and put in one of my own. I loved to see my own face and my thick black hair. Some years later, I got married. My wife was very beautiful, and I loved her a lot. I replaced my picture in this wallet with a picture of her. I spent hours gazing at her pretty face. When my first child was born, my life started a new chapter. I shortened my working hours to play with my baby. I went late to work and returned home early too. Obviously, my baby's picture occupied the prized position in my wallet."

The old man's eyes brimmed with tears as he went on. "My parents passed away many years ago. Last year my wife too left her mortal coil. My son, my only son, is too busy with his family. He has no time to look after me. All that I had ever held close to my heart is now far, far away from my reach. Now I have put this picture of Buddha in my wallet. It is only now that I have realised that he is the eternal companion. He will never leave me. Alas! If only I had realised this before. If only I had loved the Buddha all these years, with the same intensity as I loved my family, I would not have been so lonely today!"

The ticket collector quietly gave the wallet to the old man. When the train stopped at the next station, he went to a book-stall at the platform and asked the salesman, "Do you have any pictures of Buddha? I need a small one to put in my wallet!"

Patience

I remember a dinner once with Hasegawa, when somebody asked him, "How long does it take to obtain our understanding of Zen?"

He said, "It may take you three minutes; it may take you thirty years. And," he said, "I mean that."

It is that three minutes that tantalizes people! We in the West want instant results, and one of the difficulties of instant results is that they are sometimes of poor quality.

~ What is Zen? ~
~ Alan Watts ~

Faith-based and experience-based spirituality

Japanese mothers used to try to curb their children's mischief by saying, "If you aren't good, a spook will get you," or "a child snatcher will come for you."

I remember being scolded like that myself as a child. Spirituality based on faith follows a similar model of trying to guide people using certain images and ideas. On the other hand, spirituality based on experience leads people to peace by having them perceive reality clearly, thereby ridding them of fear:

Wither'd pampas grass —
that was all it really was,
the ghost that I saw.

...

Zen is at the forefront of experience-based religions. I often say that Zen is not a religion. But if salvation is considered the task of religion, it is. However, unlike faith-based religions, Zen rejects concepts and beliefs as a means of knowing the truth. Instead it aims to help us perceive reality and to find peace of mind based on that reality. Reality is what we really are: namely, our True Self. When we discover what we are, we experience peace of mind and continue to live day by day in infinite tranquillity and complete satisfaction. What more do we need?

~ Zen: The Authentic Gate ~
~ Zen Master Koun Yamada ~

I Am Here

A Man stands on top of a mountain. Other people ask Him, "Are you here for the scenery?"

The Man says: "No."

"Are you here for the fresh airs?"

The Man says. "No."

Other people then ask Him: "Then why are here?"

The Man: "Because I am here."

No-Sword Sword

A master Swordsman is very good at sword fighting. So good, at old age, He is always without a sword as He fights without a sword. His student wants to test Him, starts attacking Him. He just pulls the mat under the attacking student, and sends him falling into the river. Fight with nothing.

The Speaking Tree

Here is what Victor Frankl recounted of a meeting with a young woman in a Nazi death camp. The woman knew she was soon to die. She knew exactly what the death camp was. She was under no illusions and yet was curiously joyful. He talked with her and this is what she said: "I'm grateful fate has hit me so hard. In my former life I was spoiled, and I didn't take spiritual matters seriously." She pointed through the clouded window of the hut to a chestnut tree, where you could just make out two blossoms on one branch. "I often talk to this tree," she told him. Frankl was startled and didn't know how to

take these words. Was she delirious? Did she have occasional hallucinations?

Anxious for her, he asked, "Does the tree reply?"

"Yes," she said.

"And what does it say to you?" he asked.

She told him, "It says to me: I am here. I am here. I am life. Eternal life."

~ Red Thread Zen: Humanly Entangled in Emptiness ~
~ By Susan Murphy ~

Resolve

Settan became a monk at the age of ten! One day he decided to go travelling to find a real guru, and he asked his mentor permission to leave. His mentor refused.

Determined to find the Way, Settan decided to go without telling anyone. Hanging a note on the temple gate saying, 'Unless I attain the Way, I will never enter this gateway again,' he left.

Finding his way to the congregation of Zen Master Torin, Settan sat in meditation day and night. Torin was one the few enlightened teachers left in those days, and his method was stern and unpredictable.

One day Settan finally decided he had no more time to waste. Climbing up to the top of a building, he vowed that he would not come down alive unless he attained enlightenment that night.

Sitting in deep meditation, all through the night, by dawn Settan had not broken through. Getting up in disgust he went to the railing to jump off the building to his death.

All of a sudden, just as he was about to step over, he heard a cock crow. At that moment Settan's mind opened up and he was greatly enlightened.

Overwhelmed with joy, Settan hurried to the teacher. When Master Torrin saw him, he at once affirmed, "You have broken through".

The Window

Two men, both seriously ill, occupied the same hospital room. One man was allowed to sit up in his bed for an hour each afternoon to help drain the fluid from his lungs. His bed was next to the room's only window. The other man had to spend all his time flat on his back. The men talked for hours on end. They spoke of their wives and families, their homes, their jobs, their involvement in the military service, where they had been on holiday.

And every afternoon when the man in the bed by the window could sit up, he would pass the time by describing to his roommate all the things he could see outside the window. The man in the other bed began to live for those one-hour periods where his world would be broadened and enlivened by all the activity and colour of the world outside.

The window overlooked a park with a lovely lake. Ducks and swans played on the water while children sailed their model boats. Young lovers walked arm in arm amidst flowers of every colour of the rainbow. Grand old trees graced the landscape and a fine view of the city skyline could be seen in the distance.

As the man by the window described all this in exquisite detail, the man on the other side of the room would close his eyes and imagine the picturesque scene.

One warm afternoon the man by the window described a parade passing by. Although the other man couldn't hear the band - he could see it in his mind's eye as the gentleman by the window portrayed it with descriptive words. Days and weeks passed.

One morning, the day nurse arrived to bring water for their baths only to find the lifeless body of the man by the window, who had died peacefully in his sleep. She was saddened and called the hospital attendants to take the body away. As soon as it seemed appropriate, the other man asked if he could be moved next to the window. The nurse was happy to make the switch and, after making sure he was comfortable, she left him alone. Slowly, painfully, he propped himself up on one elbow to take his first look at the world outside. Finally, he would have the joy of seeing it for himself. He strained to slowly turn to look out the window beside the bed.

It faced a blank wall. The man asked the nurse what could have compelled his deceased roommate who had described such wonderful things outside this window. The nurse responded that the man was blind and could not even see the wall. She said, "Perhaps he just wanted to encourage you."

Sitting in a dark room without becoming inattentive

At first Zen Master Hongzhi [1091-1157] was the attendant of Chun of Da Once, when Hongzhi was inquiring about a koan with some other monks, he unknowingly laughed out loud. Chun scolded him saying, "How many good things you have lost by this laugh! Haven't you seen the saying, "If you are absent even for a moment, you are the same as a dead man'?"

Hongzhi bowed in homage and took what Chun said to heart. Thereafter even when he was in a dark room, he never dared to be inattentive.

Dream

The lady Li Chi was the daughter of Ai Feng. When the Duke of Chin first got her, she wept until the bosom of her dress was drenched with tears. But when she came to the royal residence, and lived with the Duke, and ate rich food, she repented of having wept. How then do I know but that the dead repent of having previously clung to life?

Those who dream of the banquet wake to lamentation and sorrow. Those who dream of lamentation and sorrow wake to join the hunt. While they dream, they do not know that they dream. Some will even interpret the very dream they are dreaming; and only when they awake do they know it was a dream. By and by comes the Great Awakening, and then we find out that this life is really a great dream. Fools think they are awake now and flatter themselves they know if they are really princes or peasants. Confucius and you are both dreams; and I who say you are dreams, --I am but a dream myself. This is a paradox. Tomorrow a sage may arise to explain it; but that tomorrow will not be until ten thousand generations have gone by.

~ Zhuangzi ~

Kill the Buddha

Shumpo Soki
(Died on the fourteenth day of the first month, 1496 at the age of eighty-eight)

My sword leans against the sky.
With its polished blade I'll behead
The Buddha and all of his saints.
Let the lightning strike where it will.

It is said that after reciting this poem, Shumpo gave a single "laugh of derision" and died. To "behead The Buddha" suggests spiritual independence and an awareness freed from the manner of thought dictated by religious tradition. According to Buddhist belief, a man who sins against religion and morality is liable to die by a stroke of lightning.

~ Book: Japanese Death Poems ~
~ Yoel Hoffmann ~

The Eleventh Hour

Chosha used to come to participate in the special annual intensive meditation session with Zen master Hakuin every single year, yet he never attained anything.

Finally, one-year Hakuin said to him at the conclusion of the session: "You come here every year, just like a duck diving into the water when it is cold. You are making a long journey in vain, without gaining half a bit of empowerment. I can't imagine how many straw sandals you have worn out over the years making this trip. I have no use for idlers like you around here, so don't come anymore!"

Deeply stirred, Chosha thought to himself, "Am I not a man? If I do not penetrate through to realization this time, I will never return home alive. I will concentrate on meditation until I die."

Setting himself a limit of seven days, Chosha went to sit in a fishnet shed by the seashore. but even after seven days of sitting in meditation without eating or sleeping, Chosha was still at a loss. There was nothing for him to do but drown himself in the ocean. Removing his shoes in the traditional manner of a suicide rite, Chosha stood in the waves. At that moment, seeing the shimmering ocean and the rising sun merging into a crimson radiance, all at once he became completely empty and greatly awakened.

~ Sayings: The Wisdom of Zen ~
~ Manuela Dunn Mascetti ~

Does Zen teach belief in God?

Two elderly Baptist ladies knocked at my door to inquire whether I believed in God. I assured them that I did, and they left satisfied. It was only after they'd gone that I realized I could, without contradicting myself, have just as well answered "No," or "Don't know," or even "Don't care." Zen is a way of liberation. It rejects all concepts, even that of "God." Once you name something, you limit it. Zen knows no limits. In fact, if you want Zen, be quick and throw it away!

~ Zen Questions ~
~ Robert Allen ~

Attained

Wu-an (Gottan: 1197—1276), the Chinese Zen master, under whom Tokiyori had his final enlightenment after twenty-one years of constant application, composed the following verse for his illustrious disciple:

I have no Buddhism about which I can this moment talk to you.

Nor have you any mind with which you listen to me hoping for an attainment:

Where there is neither preaching nor attainment nor mind.

There Shakyamuni has a most intimate interview with Buddha Dipankara.

After a very successful regency. Tokiyori died in 1263. when he was only thirty-seven years old. When he realized that the time for departure was approaching, he put on his Buddhist robe and sat on a straw seat of meditation. After writing his farewell song, he passed away quietly. The song reads:

The karma mirror raised high,

These thirty-seven years!

'Tis broken now with one hammer blow.

The Great Way remains ever serene!

~ Zen and Japanese Culture ~
~ D.T. Suzuki ~

Zen and the Dawn of the Truth

Genro traveled all over Japan visiting Zen Masters from time he was nineteen years old. Eventually he thought to himself, 'The teachers everywhere are alike, giving guidance at random. They are unreliable. If I remain in a community, I will waste a lot of time on trivial things. It would be better me if I lived alone in a deserted place in order to meditate single-mindedly.'

One afternoon as he watched the setting sun, Genro sighed to himself, 'I have already spent five years working on Zen day and night. If I just spend my days this way, when will I ever pass all the way through?'

Genro then sat on a boulder and plunged into intense concentration. Without realizing it, he sat there all through the night. Unaware of the breaking of dawn. Genro suddenly heard the bell of a distant temple. At that moment, his mind opened up and he attained great enlightenment.

Twenty-four years old at the time, Genro composed an ex-tempore verse on this happy occasion:

At dawn, in response to the temple bell, the universe opens,
  The orb of the sun, bright, comes from the Great East.
  What this principle is, I do not know.
  Unawares my jowls are filled with gales of laughter.

Zen Cannot Be Said

One day, a student asks the Zen Master to give a class. The Zen Master says, "Ok. Please gather all the students." When all the students gather for the class. The Zen Master just leaves without saying a word. When asked why, the Zen Master replied, "Zen cannot be said." Zen cannot be said, it is just to know.

The Teaching

Once it happened: A man came to a Zen master and asked to be taught. The master said, "Okay. You be here, and I will teach you." The man remained for one, two, three hours, then his patience came to an end.

Many people were coming and going. Many people were asking many questions – the master had many disciples, a great monastery, and he was talking to people, teaching people, giving them methods, solving their problems – and the man was sitting in the corner. He became very impatient, almost feverish.

When he could get a time he said, "Wait. I have been here for three hours and you have not taught me anything!"

The master looked at him and said, "What have I been doing the whole time? People came, they asked me questions, I answered. There was teaching in it – not in the answer but in the answering.

You should have watched how I answered. People came, they greeted me, I responded. There was teaching. And sometimes people came, and they simply sat by my side in silence, and I was silent, they were silent – there was teaching for you.

What have I been doing for these three hours, you fool! I have been teaching you." But the man was at a loss. He couldn't understand what type of teaching this was.

A master does not teach, he IS the teaching. His whole being is a message, a continuous message. The way he moves his eyes, the way he gestures, the way he looks at you – something is there continuously being conveyed. And if you cannot see you are blind.

~ Osho: Just Like That ~

Asking

A monk asked, "The point of asking a question-what is it?"
Joshu said, "Mistake."
The monk asked, "The point of asking no questions-what about that?"
Joshu said, "You can see it in my previous word."

~ Case 264 of Radical Zen ~

How Long?

There is an Indian story of a marvellous medicine that could cure all ills. However, it only worked if you didn't think of a monkey when you swallowed it.

If you think about enlightenment, you can never attain it. It is not a prize that you can win.

~ Zen Questions ~
~ Robert Allen ~

Buddha's Statement

Two Zen-men were discussing Zen. One, named Chokei (Ch'ang-ch'ing Huiding, 853—932) , said, "Even a fully enlightened arhat may be proclaimed to be still harboring something of the three poisonous passions (Greed, Anger and Folly),' but as to the Buddha, he never makes an equivocal statement. Whatever he asserts is absolute truth. What do you say to this?"

Hofuku (Pao-fu Ts'ung-chan, d. 928) asked, "What then is the Buddha's statement?"

Chokei said, "The deaf cannot hear it."

This was criticized by Hofuku: "You are coming down onto a secondary level."

"What then is the Buddha's statement according to your judgment?"

"Have a cup of tea, 0 my brother-monk. "

~ Zen and Japanese Culture ~
~ D.T. Suzuki ~

Buddha

A student asks, "What is Buddha?"
The master replies, "There never was one!"

~ Zen and Us ~
~ Jarkfrued Graf Durckheim ~

Gatha (Death Poem)

One of the most traditional forms of Zen art is the death poem or "gatha" – a stanza of four lines which Zen masters would write to summarize their teaching for their students shortly before assuming the cross-legged zazen position and passing on. Here is how some of them handled this auspicious moment:

"What shall be my legacy?
The blossoms of spring,
The cuckoo in the hills,
The leaves of autumn."

~ Ryokan (1758-1831) ~
~ Book: Zen Beginners ~

The Way

"What is the way?"
"Go!"

~ Book: Zen Beginners ~

Iron Face

Buttsu and Genro were known throughout Japan as two of the fiercest Zen Masters in the land. They were so ferocious in the ways, they handled seekers that they were called Genro the Wolf and Buttsu the Tiger.

Nobody knows where Buttsu came from or what his original name was. Some say he was originally a warrior from eastern Japan. He studied Zen for a long time and finally completed the great Work. In his verse, on awakening, he wrote:

This matter has been on my mind for eighteen years;
how many times have I gotten power
yet still could not sleep at peace?
One call, one answer and clarity is complete;
I have vomited out the bellly-ful of Zen
that I had learned before!

Battsu has a face of iron, severe and cold. He trained Zen students with harsh methods, not allowing human feelings to enter into the process at all. Many seekers who came to him could not bear this and left.

In the middle of the night of his death, Buttsu looked

around and said, 'Shall I go now?' Then he passed away, while sitting in meditation, as though he had fallen asleep.

Instruction

Tokusan Zenji, who was famous for his use of the stick in instruction, ranks with Rinzai as one of the most severe of the outstanding Zen teachers. It is said that no matter what question was brought to him, he responded with, "Tell me and I'll give you thirty blows; fail to tell me and I'll give you thirty blows!" He was a true master in using the stick to "kill" his students and "bring them back to life" again.

~ Zen: The Authentic Gate ~
~ Zen Master Koun Yamada ~

Three years of energetic practice

Zen Master Zuxin of Huitang [1025-1100) would say of himself, "When I first entered the Path, it was very easy to go my own way. Then when I met my late teacher Huanglong, I reflected back on my daily activities and saw that thwre were many contradictions between my conduct and the principles of the Budhist Path. So, I practiced the Path energetically for three years, through the bitter cold and stifling heat, without wavering from my true intent. Only then did I get so that everything was in accord with the principles of the Path. Now even when I cough and spit or shrug my shoulders, it is all the essential meaning the Zen transmission."

Heaven and Hell

A woman who had worked all her life to bring about good was granted one wish: "Before I die let me visit both hell and heaven." Her wish was granted.

She was whisked off to a great banqueting hall. The tables were piled high with delicious food and drink. Around the tables sat miserable, starving people as wretched as could be. "Why are they like this?" she asked the angel who accompanied her. "Look at their arms," the angel replied. She looked and saw that attached to the people's arms were long chopsticks secured above the elbow. Unable to bend their elbows, the people aimed the chopsticks at the food, missed every time and sat hungry, frustrated and miserable. "Indeed, this is hell! Take me away from here!"

She was then whisked off to heaven. Again, she found herself in a great banqueting hall with tables piled high. Around the tables sat people laughing, contented, joyful. "No chopsticks I suppose," she said. "Oh yes there are. Look - just as in hell they are long and attached above the elbow but look... here people have learnt to feed one another".

Worth

A father before he died said to his son: "This is a watch your grandfather gave me and is more than 200 years old. But before I give it to you, go to the watch shop on the first street, and tell him I want to sell it, and see how much he offers you".

He went, and then came back to his father, and said, "the watchmaker offered 5 dollars because it's old".

He said to him: "Go to the coffee shop".

He went and then came back and said: "He offered $5 father".

"Go to the museum and show that watch".

He went then came back and said to his father "They offered me a million dollars for this piece".

The father said: "I wanted to let you know that the right place values you in right way. Don't find yourself in the wrong place and get angry if you are not valued. Those that know your value are those who appreciate you, don't stay in a place where nobody sees your value".

Know your worth.

Precepts

The Vinaya (literally "the discipline," the "leading out") is the 227 disciplinary rules and renunciations intended to form and conform the conduct of male monastic life, and the even more ramified and numerous 311 rules apparently required by the innate unruliness of female monastics.

A young man heard about this formidable set of regulations and asked a Chinese nun, "How on earth do you manage to keep all 311 precepts?"

She replied, "I keep only one precept."

The young man, shocked, asked, "What is that?"

"I just watch my mind," she said.

~ Red Thread Zen: Humanly Entangled in Emptiness ~
~ By Susan Murphy ~

Road to Enlightenment

A student monk: "The road to Enlightenment starts from where?"

Zen Master uses his stick to draw a line on the soil in front of the student monk: "The road starts here." Zen starts here.

Fearless

A classic Zen story about their fearlessness is the tale of a young man who applied to a fencing master to be his student. The master looked at him and said, "Who did you study with before?"

He said, "I've never studied fencing before."

The master looked at him in a funny way and said, "No, surely, come now, you have studied with someone."

He said, "No sir, I never have studied."

"Well," the master said, "I'm an experienced teacher, and I can tell at once by looking at a person whether he has studied fencing or not. And I know you have!"

But the young man shook his head and said, "Sir, I assure you, I've never studied fencing at all with anybody."

"Well," said the master, "there must be something peculiar about you — what do you suppose it could be?"

"Well," the young man said, "when I was a boy, I was very worried about dying. So, I thought a great deal about death. And then I came to the realization that there's nothing in death to be afraid of."

"Oh," said the master, "that explains it."

~ What is Zen? ~
~ Alan Watts ~

Thus Reached

Ishida Baigan was a founder of Shingaku Mind Studies, a lay movement inspired by Zen. Up until the time he was fifty years old, it is said, displeasure used to show on Baigan's face whenever something offended him. After the age of fifty, however, he never evinced any sign of pleasure or displeasure. When he reached the age of sixty, he said, "Now I have attained ease."

~ Zen Antics ~
~ Thomas Cleary ~

Stern Measures

Izu studied Zen with Hakuin for a long time. As a teacher in his own right, Izu inherited the harsh manner of the redoubtable master Hakuin but was even sterner. Whenever he would receive people asking about Zen, he would lay a naked sword next to his seat. If they were hesitant or argumentative, he would chase them out with the sword.

An Awakening

Zen Master Setsugen told his student Jijo, 'If you meditate single-mindedly without interruption for seven days and nights, and yet still do not attain realization, you can cut off my head and my skull into a nightsoil scoop.'

No longer after that, Jijo came down with a case of dysentery. Taking a bucket to a secluded placed, he sat on it and held his attention in right mindfulness.

When he had sat on the bucket for seven straight days, one night he suddenly sensed the whole world like snowy landscape under bright moon light and felt as if the entire universe were too small to contain him.

He had been absorbed in this state for a long time when he was startled into self-awareness on hearing a sound. He found his whole body running with a sweat and his sickness had disappeared. In celebration, he wrote a verse:

Radiant, spiritual ---- what is this?
The minute you blink your eyes you've missed it.
The spatula by the toilet shines with light;
After all it was just me all along.

Contentment

Kansan left home when he was nine years old. He had a brilliant mind and studied both Buddhist and Confucian classics. Inspired by one of the books he read, for a time Kansan devoted himself to the study and practice of esoteric Buddhism in western Japan. Later he went to the capital city of Edo, where he perused the massive Buddhist canon.

After nearly two decades of these studies, Kansan finally went to see a Zen Master. Well versed in Buddhist practices, Kansan mastered the Zen teachings in two years of intensive work.

Subsequently Kansan was sent to take over the abbacy of a temple in southern Japan. When he arrived, he found that drinking and carousing were so common in the area, that the temple itself was accustomed to supplying visitors with wine, as if it were a lounge.

On the day that Kansan finally took over the abbacy of the temple, he destroyed every single wine jar, ashtray, and serving table. After that guests were treated with a single cup of plain tea.

Three years later, Kansan retired. He disappeared into the

mountains, putting a sign over the door of his hunt, that simply said, 'CONTENT."

Two Frogs in the Milk

This is the story of two frogs. One frog was fat and the other skinny. One day, while searching for food, they inadvertently jumped into a vat of milk. They couldn't get out, as the sides were too slippery, so they were just swimming around.

The fat frog said to the skinny frog, "Brother frog, there's no use paddling any longer. We're just going to drown, so we might as well give up." The skinny frog replied, "Hold on brother, keep paddling. Somebody will get us out." And they continued paddling for hours.

After a while, the fat frog said, "Brother frog, there's no use. I'm becoming very tired now. I'm just going to stop paddling and drown. It's Sunday and nobody's working. We're doomed. There's no possible way out of here." But the skinny frog said, "Keep trying. Keep paddling. Something will happen, keep paddling." Another couple of hours passed.

The fat frog said, "I can't go on any longer. There's no sense in doing it because we're going to drown anyway. What's the use?" And the fat frog stopped. He gave up. And he drowned in the milk. But the skinny frog kept on paddling.

Ten minutes later, the skinny frog felt something solid beneath his feet. He had churned the milk into butter, and he hopped out of the vat.

~ Author: Melissa D Zartman ~

The Tao

In the days when Zen Master Yakusan (751-834) was still actively instructing his disciples, Rikoh - the governor of Ho-Shu and a great Confucian - went to visit Yakusan, whom he greatly admired. Yakusan was looking at a sutra when the attendant monk showed Rikoh into the master's room. Yakusan did not look up at the governor's arrival, but he appeared absorbed in what he was reading.

After a few moments, Rikoh, who had a hot temper, could not stand it anymore. He grumbled, "It's better to hear your name than to see your face," and stood up to leave.

Immediately Yakusan said, "Why do you respect the ear and look down on the eye?"

Rikoh pressed his hands together and bowed down. He then asked, "Could you please tell me what the Tao is?"

Yakusan immediately pointed up and then down with his hand and asked, "Do you understand?"

Rikoh said, "I don't understand."

Yakusan shouted, "Clouds are in the sky, water is in the well!"

Rikoh suddenly realized and felt great joy. And with his

contentment, he bowed down to Yakusan and presented this poem to him:

Achieved form, it looks like a form of the crane.

Under the thousands of pine trees, the way of the two poles.

I come and ask Tao: no wasteful argument.

Clouds are in the sky; water is in the well.

~ Sayings: The Wisdom of Zen ~
~ Manuela Dunn Mascetti ~

Zen Dialogue

The pupil asks, "What is everyday living?"
The master raises his fly whisk.
"Is that it?" inquires the monk.
"What is that?" says the master.
The monk makes no answer.

~ Zen and Us ~
~ Jarkfrued Graf Durckheim ~

So Unnatural

In one story, [Zen Master] Sosan [1520-1604] and [his student] Samyong were taking a walk through the mountains, and Sosan was slightly ahead. Samyong took an appraising look at his teacher, a short, frail man of ungainly appearance. Samyong, by contrast, was a giant of a man - handsome, with a powerful presence. Struck by the contrast, Samyong could not help speculating why this physically unimpressive man should be his teacher. Soon they came to a waterfall. To his utter amazement, Samyong saw that the water of the fall was flowing upwards rather than coming down. He cried out to Sosan, "Look, this waterfall is upside down. So unnatural!" Sosan mildly replied, "Yes, just like your mind." Samyong instantly understood that Sosan had been cognizant all along of what was going through his mind and had used his magical powers to teach him. He bowed to Sosan and apologized profusely to his teacher. Sosan "released" the waterfall and the water began to come down naturally!

~ Thousand Peaks ~
~ Mu Soeng ~

The Strange Death

A Zen monk was going to die. He was very old, ninety years old. Suddenly he opened his eyes and he said, "Where are my shoes?"

And the disciple said, "Where are you going? Have you gone crazy? You are dying, and the physician has said that there is no more possibility; a few minutes more."

He said, "That's why I'm asking for my shoes: I would like to go to the cemetery, because I don't want to be dragged. I will walk on my own and I will meet death there. I don't want to be dragged. And you know me -- I have never leaned on anybody else. This will be very ugly, that four persons will be carrying me. No."

He walked to the cemetery. Not only that, he dug his own grave, lay down in it, and died.

~ Osho: The Discipline of Transcendence, Vol 4 ~

The Teaching

Someone said, "I have come here from far away. I beg you to teach me."

Joshu said, "You have just entered the gate. Well then, let me spit in your face."

NOTE: Why don't you look for it right where you are?

~ Case 268 of Radical Zen ~

The seeker of truth

After years of searching, the seeker was told to go to a cave, in which he would find a meditating Zen monk. 'Ask the monk what is truth', he was advised, 'and the monk will reveal it to you'. Having found the monk, the seeker asked that most fundamental question. And came the answer, 'Go to the village crossroad: there you shall find what you are seeking'.

Full of hope and anticipation the man ran to the crossroad to find only three rather uninteresting shops. One shop was selling pieces of metal, another sold wood, and thin wires were for sale in the third. Nothing and no one there seemed to have much to do with the revelation of truth.

Disappointed, the seeker returned to the monk to demand an explanation, but he was told only, 'You will understand in the future.' After saying this, the monk closed his eyes and went in deep meditation. Indignant for having been made a fool of - or so he thought at the time - the seeker continued his wanderings in search of truth. As years went by, the memory of his experience with the monk gradually faded until one night, while he was walking in the moonlight, the sound of sitar music caught his attention. It was wonderful music, and it was played with great mastery and inspiration.

Profoundly moved, the truth seeker felt drawn towards the player. He looked at the fingers dancing over the strings. He became aware of the sitar itself. And then suddenly he exploded in a cry of joyous recognition: the sitar was made out of wires and pieces of metal and wood just like those he had once seen in the three stores and had thought it to be without any particular significance.

At last, he understood the message of the monk: we have already been given everything we need: our task is to assemble and use it in the appropriate way. Nothing is meaningful so long as we perceive only separate fragments. But as soon as the fragments come together into a synthesis, a new entity emerges, whose nature we could not have foreseen by considering the fragments alone.

Importance of Zen

As a young Zen student, Richard Baker habitually used to come just barely in time for zazen in San Francisco. His teacher Shunryu Suzuki casually said to him once, "You must have many important things to do." After that Baker was never even close to being late.

~ Essential Zen ~
~ Edited by Kazuaki Tenahashi and Tensho David Schneider ~

The Failed Monk

A Zen monk named Ichhi labored his whole life in the kitchen of the great monastery at Lake Hakkone. He was deemed a "failed monk" by himself and his superiors because he had been assigned the koan of "What is the sound of one hand clapping?" since his earliest days in the congregation and had never been able to solve it. It was now fifty-five years of failure and he was nearing the end of his life-time.

But as he lay dying, he suddenly realized that he cradled a great peace in his soul. Gone was the striving for enlightenment, gone was the stridency of his loins, and gone was the haunting koan - for he had found the stillness of no longer striving in this exquisite silence alone in the attic in the soft dark at the end of his life.

It was only then, when there remained no more questions nor need for answers (or even the need for breathing) that Ichhi heard at last the whooshing silence of one hand clapping.

~ Zen Fables for Today ~
~ Richard McLean ~

No Scriptures

The Twenty-seventh Patriarch was called Prajnatara, and it is said that he was once invited to the religious assembly of a king in Eastern India. Noticing that the distinguished guest did not occupy himself all the time in reading the scriptures as did the others, the king asked him," What is this not reading of the Sutras?"

" The poor man's path," was the reply. He also said," When breathing in, dis-identifying oneself with mind, with sense-activity, with empirical consciousness, with conceptions, with making judgments. Breathing out, not being entangled in the mass of external relations. When it is done, verily the Sutras are being read-hundreds, thousands, millions of volumes!"

~ Trevor Leggett ~

The Present Moment

"What is the present moment?"
"No one ever asked me that before."
"I am asking now, master."
"You fool!"

~ Zen and Us ~
~ Jarkfrued Graf Durckheim ~

Do ordinary people experience Zen?

A boy was racked with teenage angst. He worried about school, he worried about his parents, he worried about going to university, he worried about the state of the world, and he worried because he had no girlfriend, and all his friends did. One day he worried himself to such a pitch that he simply ran out of the ability to worry any more. A beautiful calm descended upon him. He looked around the familiar living room of his parents' house and his gaze was arested by a wastepaper basket made of plaited palm leaves. To his amaze-ment this humble object, that would normally rate only the briefest glance, now seemed utterly transformed. It wasn't that the basket had changed physically. It wasn't glowing or burning, but it was infused with an inner glow like nothing he had ever seen before. It was only many years later that he real-ized this was his first step in Zen.

~ Zen Questions ~
~ Robert Allen ~

What to believe?

Gyozan said to Sekishitsu, "Tell me what to believe in and what to rely on?"

Sekishitsu gestured across the sky above, three times with his hand, and said, "There is no such thing."

Gyozan asked, "What do you say about reading sutras?"

Sekishitsu replied, "All the sutras are out of the question. Doing things that are given by others is dualism of mind and matter. And if you are in the dualism of subject and object, various views arise. But this is blind wisdom, so it is not yet the Tao.

"If others don't give you anything, there is not a single thing. That's why Bodhidharma said, 'Originally, there is not a single thing.'

"You see, when a baby comes out of the womb, does he read sutras or not? At that time, the baby doesn't know whether such a thing as buddha nature exists or not. As he grows up and learns various views, he appears to the world and says, 'I do well, and I understand.' But he doesn't know it is rubbish and delusion.

"Of the sixteen ways or phases of doing, a baby's way is

the best. The time of a baby's gurgle is compared to a seeker when he leaves the mind of dividing and choosing. That's why a baby is praised. But if you take this comparison and say, 'The baby is the way,' people of the present days will understand it wrongly."

~ Sayings: The Wisdom of Zen ~
~ Manuela Dunn Mascetti ~

The Tortoise in The Mud

CHUANG Tzu was fishing in the P'u when the prince of Ch'u sent two high officials to ask him to take charge of the administration of the Ch'u State.

Chuang Tzu went on fishing and, without turning his head, said "I have heard that in Ch'u there is a sacred tortoise which has been dead now some three thousand years, and that the prince keeps this tortoise carefully enclosed in a chest on the altar of his ancestral temple. Now would this tortoise rather be dead and have its remains venerated, or be alive and wagging its tail in the mud?"

"It would rather be alive," replied the two officials, "and wagging its tail in the mud."

"Begone!" cried Chuang Tzu. "I too will wag my tail in the mud."

~ Zhuangzi ~

Dogen's Enlightenment

Dogen Zenji studied under Nyojō Zenji for more than two years, devoting himself to selfless practice toward the final goal of all Zen students.

One night, during the predawn sitting period, Nyojō Zenji came upon a monk dozing on his cushion. With an unusually stern voice he rebuked the monk, "In the practice of Zen, body and mind must fall away. What are you doing sleeping?"

When Dogen, who was sitting in the zendo, heard the words "body and mind must fall away," he was suddenly enlightened. He forgot himself completely. He jumped up and followed Nyojō Zenji to his room, where he lit incense and prostrated himself before his master.

"Why are you lighting incense?" Nyojō Zenji asked.

Dogen Zenji replied, "Body and mind have fallen away."

Nyojō Zenji said, "Body and mind fallen away; fallen away body and mind" — words of confirmation.

Dogen Zenji, scrupulous to the end, said, "It is but a momentary occurrence. Please do not bestow the seal of approval upon me lightly."

"I do not confirm you without reason," Nyojō said as he reconfirmed him. Nyojō Zenji had an unerring eye.

"Why do you say that you do not confirm me without reason?" asked Dogen.

Nyojō Zenji then gave his final seal of approval, saying, "Fallen away body and mind."

~ Zen: The Authentic Gate ~
~ Zen Master Koun Yamada ~

Zen

"What is Zen?"
"Boiling oil over a blazing fire."

~ Masao Abe: A Zen Life of Dialogue ~

The Last Porridge

YAKUO TOKUKEN
(Died on the nineteenth day of the fifth month, 1320 at the age of seventy-six)

My six and seventy years are through.
I was not born; I am not dead.
Clouds floating on the high wide skies
The moon curves through its million-mile course.

Two days before his death, Yakuo called his fellow monks together and said, "The words of a man before he dies are no small matter. This is a barrier that all must pass through. Tell me each of you what you think about that."

The monks answered in various ways, and Yakuo neither approved nor disapproved. The next day he ordered his pupils to burn his body and forbade them to hold an elaborate burial ceremony.

"Tomorrow morning," he said, "I shall eat the rice porridge with you for breakfast, and at noon I shall go. The following day at noon he wrote his final words, threw the brush from his hand, and died sitting upright.

~ Book: Japanese Death Poems ~
~ Yoel Hoffmann ~

Nothingness

An abbess practicing Zen speaks to her disciples during their meditations: "How is it with nothingness?"

"I don't know," replies a young man who had been able to endure the difficulties of Zen practice only with great effort.

"How is it with nothingness?" the abbess asked again, hitting him on the legs with a stick.

At the moment he is struck, an exclamation of enlightenment bursts from the disciple's mouth: " Suddenly I feel that it has become bright. Oh, it is nothingness, this is nothingness, and that is nothingness."

~ Zen: The Reason of Unreason ~

Supernatural Powers

A young man wished to acquire supernatural powers. After a long search for a teacher, he found a Mountain Immortal who consented to teach him on condition that he never asked about or interfered with whatever he might see. The eager young man agreed. He saw a dog beated badly, and then a man - but he firmly kept his mouth shut and looked the other way. Finally, his instructor took him down to hell with him. There he saw both his father and mother dragged forward in chains, and fiends beating them. At that he sprang forward: 'No! stop!' And found himself back in his home village, content, and no longer lusting after supernatural powers.

~ The Wisdom of the Zen masters ~
~ Irmgard Schloegl ~

Not Yet

There was a Zen student under a master to whom he was very much devoted. Each time he approached the master, the latter waved his hand, saying, "Not yet, not yet." Some time passed. One evening he became desperate: "How can this be? I have no word of instruction which will lead me to the realisation. The master simply chases me, saying, 'Not yet, not yet.' What can I do? What do I have to think about it all?"

He went on like this in utter desperation, but tenaciously clinging to his object of inquiry and pondering it from every possible point of view, when all of a sudden something flashed on his mind and he realised at once what the master wanted him to discover. The following morning, he visited the master, wishing to let him know what happened to him. But the aster seeing him come burst out, "You have it now, you have it now!"

~ What is Zen? ~
~ D.T. Suzuki ~

A Round headrest to prevent dozing off

Attendant Zhe [d. 1095] used a round piece of wood as a headrest. When he began to doze off, the headrest would roll, and he would be awakened and get up again. He did this most of the time and made it his constant practice. Someone said to him that he was overtaxing his mind, but he answered: "My affinity with transcendent wisdom is slight: if I do not act like this, I am afraid I will be dragged off by false habits."

Transcended

Someone asked, "Who has transcended heaven and earth?" Joshu said, "If you come across such a one, let me know immediately. "

~ Case 276 of Radical Zen ~

The Essential Sound of Emptiness

The disciple approaches the master and asks, "What is the essential sound of emptiness?"

The master replies, "What is the essential sound of emptiness?"

"You are the master. I don't know the answer, that's why I'm asking."

The master strikes him on the head. The disciple becomes enlightened.

~ The Finger and the Moon: Zen Teachings and Koans ~
~ Alejandro Jodorowsky ~

The Way

Someone asked, "The Way of the monk-what is it?"
Joshu said, "Being detached from 'the Way.'"

~ Case 350 of Radical Zen ~

Asan's Rooster

JAPAN, EIGHTEENTH CENTURY

ASAN WAS a laywoman who studied Zen with Master Tetsumon and was unremitting in her devotion to practice.

One day during her morning sitting she heard the crow of the rooster and her mind suddenly opened. She spoke a verse in response:

The fields, the mountains, the flowers,
and my body too
are the voice of the bird —
what is left that can be said to hear?

Master Tetsumon recognized her enlightenment.

~ The Hidden Lamp: Stories from Twenty-Five Centuries of Awakened Women ~

~ Zoketsu Norman Fischer ~

Asan's Dewdrop

JAPAN, EIGHTEENTH CENTURY

ASAN WAS a lay student of the Soto Zen master Tetsumon and was greatly enlightened. Later, she also met with Hakuin.

In her old age, Asan became seriously ill and her sons and daughters gathered around her, seeking some last words.

Asan laughed and said: "In this world where not even a drop of dew on a

leaf of a word remains, what sort of saying should I leave?" Then she serenely passed away.

~ The Hidden Lamp: Stories from Twenty-Five Centuries
of Awakened Women ~
~ Zoketsu Norman Fischer ~

Got 'It'!

Chinul (1158-1210) was one of the most important figures in Korean Zen. He was sickly as a child, and his father vowed that if his son's health improved, he would have him ordained as a monk. The boy accordingly entered a Zen monastery when he was seven and was ordained at the age of fifteen. he does not seem to have had a permanent teacher or ever to have received transmission in a lineage, displaying rather a penchant for self-reliance and seclusion and developing his practice using the sutras and the works of Chinese Zen Masters as guidelines. It was when he was reading a passage from the Platform Sutra on the freedom and self-reliance of true nature that he had his first enlightenment experience. Later, while searching the Hua-yen Sutra for a passage confirming the approach of Zen, he had a profound awakening when he read: "As one particle of dust contains thousands of sutras, so the wisdom of all Buddhas is complete in the bodies of ordinary people who do not realize it."

~ Zen Sourcebook: Traditional Documents from China, Korea, Japan ~

~ Edited by Stephen Addiss ~

Nothing

One spring evening, Muso Soseki was meditating under a tree outside his hermitage. When it was fully night, he stood up to return to the hut. Because it was too dark for him to be able to see, he reached out to where he thought the hermitage wall should be. There was nothing there, and he stumbled and fell. At that moment, it was as if he had fallen through a "wall of darkness" into light. The "unity of all things" was no longer a concept but rather an achieved experience. He wrote this verse to commemorate the event:

For many years I dug the earth and searched for the blue heaven,

And how often, how often did my heart grow heavier and heavier.

One night, in the dark, I took stone and brick,

And mindlessly struck the bones of the empty heavens.

~ Zen Masters of Japan ~

Chaoyan

CHAOYAN was born in Hangzhou, in present-day Zhejiang province, to the Qiu family. She appears to have been raised in a monastery setting, leaving home when she was only three years old — we do not know if this was because of her spiritual precocity, or perhaps because her parents were poor and could not afford to raise her. She was tonsured when she was only eleven years old and subsequently became the disciple of Chan master Benchong Sheng (d.1671), who was a Dharma heir of Feiyin Tongrong and the abbot of the Huiyun Monastery in Hangzhou. She appears to have been quite famous for her literary gifts: there is mention of a collection of her recorded sayings, which I have been unable to locate. The seventeenth-century woman anthologist Wang Duanshu writes that "When I read all the poems in her recorded sayings, [I find them to be like] fish leaping in the vast sea, [like] birds soaring in the heavens above. They are neither separated from words nor obstructed by words."

A Self-Description
Above the highest peak of Mount Wu,

the round moon is alone,
Cold and bland, pure and poor,
it does not possess a single thing.
If someone should come along and ask
what this nun is doing,
She sits for long hours on her meditation mat
enjoying herself.

Meditation Mat Gatha
On this mat I've silently sat in solitary meditation retreat,
Four years come and gone; my old countenance has changed.
In a snap of the fingers I've seen through the mind's games,
The blue mountains stand as before among the white clouds.

Summer Rains
Thousands of trees are swaying in the wind and driving rain,
Whistling fiercely by my couch as the first watch draws near.
Tossing in my bed, a cool dream scatters just like the clouds
As the moon rises in the western sky in a thin shaft of light.

~ Daughters of Emptiness ~
~ Beata Grant ~

Take Care!

A Master gardener, famous for his skill in climbing and pruning the highest trees, examined his disciple by letting him climb a very high tree. Many people had come to watch. The master gardener stood quietly, carefully following every move but not interfering with one word. Having pruned the top, the disciple climbed down and was only about ten feet from the ground when the master suddenly yelled: 'Take care, take care!'

When the disciple was safely down an old man asked the master gardener: 'You did not let out one word when he was aloft in the most dangerous place. Why did you caution him when he was nearly down? Even if he had slipped then, he could not have greatly hurt himself.'

'But isn't it obvious?' replied the master gardener. 'Right up at the top he is conscious of the danger, and of himself takes care. But near the end when one begins to feel safe, this is when accidents occur.

~ The Wisdom of the Zen masters ~
~ Irmgard Schloegl ~

The Buddha Abused

The Buddha had a lay disciple who often neglected his wife in order to go listen to the Buddha preach. This made his wife feel very lonely, and very angry. She was angry not only with her husband, but also with the Buddha. She believed that the Buddha was using some mystical power to steal her husband. One day, after her husband had come home late the night before, she went to the Buddha to speak her mind. She yelled at him and abused him with very harsh words. The Buddha sat listening quietly, without speaking. The disciples did not like to hear the Master addressed with such language and tried to push the woman away. The Buddha made them stop. The woman continued upbraiding the Buddha for a time and then left without saying good-bye. After she left, the disciples asked the Buddha why he did not answer her back. The Buddha said:

"Let me ask you first. If somebody were to offer you a pleasing gift, what would you do?"

"We would accept it, Lord."

"if somebody were to offer you a disagreeable gift, what would you do?"

"We would not accept it, Lord."

"If you did not accept it, what would become of it?"

"It would remain in the owner's hands."

The Buddha continued: "Now just that has happened with the woman who was here. She offered me a disagreeable gift, and I did not accept it. So that gift is still in her hands."

~ Zen Philosophy, Zen Practice ~
~ Thich Thien-An ~

Mental

For years a rather intelligent young man suffered mental problems. He was in a clinic for some time but then they let him go. After that he went to a Zen monastery. It bothered the young man that he had been mad and that maybe he still was. He wanted to talk to the Zen master about this, but the Zen master let it pass. Worse still, the Zen master forbade anyone to speak to the young man

about his mental problems. He was only allowed to talk about the work he had to do; talk about his mental problems was ignored. The young man went to work each day, and in the mornings, when he was at work in the vegetable garden, the Zen master would walk by and ask in a friendly voice: 'Have you taken leave of your senses today?' But before the young man could answer the Zen master had already walked on. Two years later the young man led a normal life, he had a job, a wife and three children.

~ ZEN: Stories from the east ~
~ Marc Brookhuis ~

The Ultimate Teaching

For a long time, Zen Master Yaoshan had not entered the hall to give a talk. The monastery director appealed to him saying, "The community has been waiting eagerly to hear a teaching from you for quite a while."

The master said, "Well, strike the bell."

The bell was rung and the community gathered. The master ascended the teaching seat, sat there for a while, then got down and returned to his room.

The director followed after him and said, "Master you agreed to give a teaching to the community. Why didn't you offer us a single word?"

The master replied, "There are scripture teachers for scriptures, and philosophy teachers for philosophy. What do you want from this old monk?"

Go with The Flow

Two panicky city dwellers found themselves lost in the high timber. After wandering for a day and a night, they came upon an old hermit.

"How do we find our way back to civilization?" they asked the hermit.

"I could tell you, but you'd still get lost," replied the hermit.

"What should we do?" they asked.

"Go with the flow."

"I beg your pardon?"

"Go with the flow. You see that stream over there. Just follow it. Streams go into creeks and creeks go into rivers and rivers go through towns. Also, along the way you'll have water to drink and berries to eat."

"Is that what Zen people mean when they say 'go with the flow'?"

"Yes and no," replied the hermit proceeding along his way.

NOTE: "Go with the flow" is an expression that emanates

from Zen practice. Like the water in the stream we are advised to accept what life gives us as it takes to our ultimate ocean.

~ Zen Fables for Today ~
~ Richard McLean ~

Ka Ya Hiraki

Gozan (1695-1733)
(Died on the second day of the third month, 1733 at the age of thirty-eight)

Ka ya hiraki
nori toku tori no
kirabiyaka

Meaning:
Blossoms scent the air
a carefree birdsong
echoes truth.

This haiku is a kaibun poem, a palindrome in which the sequence of syllables is identical whether the poem is read from the beginning or from the end. Such a form was popular in Japanese poetry during the eighteenth and nineteenth centuries.

One source has this to say about Gozan's death:

The evening Gozan died there were still several blossoms left on the plum tree outside his window. From time to time an owl came to rest in the tree, calling, "ho, ho." Said Gozan, "My life is over...." He took up his brush and wrote his death poem.

The syllable ho is the Chinese-derived pronunciation of the character signifying "law," or "Buddha's doctrine." Gozan uses the same character with its Japanese pronunciation, nori, in his poem.

~ Book: Japanese Death Poems ~
~ Yoel Hoffmann ~

Storyteller's Zen

Encho was a famous storyteller. His tales of love stirred the hearts of his listeners. When he narrated a story of war, it was as if the listeners themselves were on the field of battle.

One day Encho met Yamaoka Tesshu, a layman who had almost embraced masterhood in Zen. "I understand," said Yamaoka, "you are the best storyteller in our land and that you make people cry or laugh at will. Tell me my favourite story of the Peach Boy. When I was a little tot I used to sleep beside my mother, and she often related this legend. In the middle of the story I would fall asleep. Tell it to me just as my mother did."

Encho dared not attempt to do this. He requested time to study. Several months later he went to Yamaoka and said: "Please give me the opportunity to tell you the story."

"Some other day," answered Yamaoka.

Encho was keenly disappointed. He studied further and tried again. Yamaoka rejected him many times. When Encho would start to talk Yamaoka would stop him, saying: "You are not yet like my mother."

It took Encho five years to be able to tell Yamaoka the legend as his mother had told it to him.

In this way, Yamaoka imparted Zen to Encho.

~ 122 Zen Koans ~

~ Taka Washi ~

Unborn

A monk was struck by the word "unborn," and that solved for him his long years of doubt. He realized his own true nature. When still a child he had been set to study a Chinese classic in which he encountered a phrase that runs "to clarify the illustrious virtue," and he became filled with doubt as to what this illustrious virtue was. A precocious child come to be aware of the problem of life at an early age. Words had to be found to represent this doubt, and the monk found them in this phrase.

To give an adequate answer to a child about his problem of life is not an easy matter. He visited many teachers, but none could satisfy him. One suggested that Zen could help him, and he started doing zazen. He must have had a natural inclination toward Zen. He continued his practice for many years without a teacher. Sometimes he went into the mountains where no one was living and spent many days on the verge of starvation. Prompted by the idea that one should ignore the body for the sake of discipline, he sat on top of a crag and never moved until he rolled down from it. Prolonged sitting caused the skin of his buttocks to break and bleed. Eventually, it seems, he became ill with tuberculosis, coughing up blood. He became weak and was on the verge of death. He thought he would not mind dying but regretted doing so without clarifying the meaning of "illustrious virtue." Members of his family prepared a cottage for him, with a servant to look after his daily needs. But his appetite was almost gone. At this stage the underground activity of the nen-thoughts must have put forth something that came up into the sphere of consciousness; suddenly the word "unborn" struck him, and everything was all right. He began to eat with an appetite and recovered his strength. Later he became a great Zen master.

~ Zen Training, Methods and Philosophy by Katsuki Sekida ~

An Impassive Old Man

A powerful warrior led his army on an invasion of a neighboring country. Since he was preceded by his reputation, nobody dared challenge him. Everyone fled his approach. One day, in a small town, he entered a temple and found inside a man of uncertain age sitting, unmoved, in lotus position.

The warrior, interpreting the motionless presence of the old man as a challenge, drew his sword.

"Do you know who you are facing, you shameless grandfather? I could pierce your heart with this sword in the blink of an eye."

Without the slightest sign of worry, the old man replied, "And you, who are you facing? I could let you pierce my heart in the blink of an eye."

~ The Finger and the Moon: Zen Teachings and Koans ~
~ Alejandro Jodorowsky ~

Why?

A monk came to see Master Gasan. Before he had even made his obeisance, the Master held out his hand asking: 'Why is this called a hand?' Then, before the monk could reply, stretched out a leg, asking: 'And why is this called a leg?' The monk opened his mouth and was about to reply when Master Gasan clapped his hands together and laughed. The startled monk withdrew without a word. Next day he came again, and Master Gasan cautioned him: 'These days Zen practitioners are given to trifling with the precious problems. Without properly disciplining themselves, they are very quick to make comments or write poems on the problems. They are no better than windbags, and not one of them would make a good teacher. If you really want Zen, give up as worthless everything you have learned and experienced. Apply yourself single-mindedly. Die and then be reborn!' At this, the monk suddenly awakened.

~ The Wisdom of the Zen masters ~
~ Irmgard Schloegl ~

Standing in the rain without noticing it

Hermit Fen was full of zeal for the Path. He had no spare time to eat or rest. One day as he was leaning on the balustrade contemplating the koan "Does a dog have buddha-nature or not?"-"No," it started to rain, but he did not notice. Only when his robe got soaked did he realize lit had been raining.

Fahai

FAHAI was from a high-ranking elite family from Hunan province: she was the aunt of a high-ranking scholar-official named Lu Jia, who was a member of the Institute of Academicians who served in the palace Hall for Treasuring Culture. Even as a young girl she was known for her intelligence, and from an early age took a special interest in the practice of Chan meditation. She became a nun and spent many years traveling from one place to another studying with various teachers, and in the end received Dharma transmission from an eminent Chan master. She then retired to a life of quiet contemplation. She attracted the attention of many eminent Confucian scholars of the day (many of whom no doubt knew of her through her nephew) who repeatedly tried to get her to leave her mountain retreat and give Chan teachings to the public. However, Fahai refused to abandon her life of quiet contemplation and remained in seclusion until her death.

Just before her death she wrote this poem and died:
On this frosty day, clouds and mist congeal,
On the mountain moon, the icy chill glows.

At night I receive a letter from my home,
At dawn I leave without anyone knowing.

~ Daughters of Emptiness ~
~ Beata Grant ~

Don't judge anyone before you know them

A 24-year-old boy seeing out from the train's window shouted...

"Dad, look the trees are going behind!"

Dad smiled and a young couple sitting nearby, looked at the 24-year old's childish behavior with pity, suddenly he again exclaimed...

"Dad, look the clouds are running with us!"

The couple couldn't resist and said to the old man, "Why don't you take your son to a good doctor?"

The old man smiled and said, "I did and we are just coming from the hospital, my son was blind from birth, he just got his eyes today."

Hua-T'ou

Here is an actual example of the questioning of a monk who was once a government official and has just started meditation:

"When you were in office, how did you protect the country and govern the people?"

The monk explains his methods of administration. Then he is asked: "Where did you get these methods?"

"From my mind."

"Where is your mind? Where is it after you die? You can't speak, you can't see, you lie there for three days and begin to stink. Where is it?"

The monk tries in vain to explain where his mind is and the instructor sends him back to the meditation hall to work on that as his hua-t'ou.

~ The Practice of Chinese Buddhism ~
~ Holmes Welch ~

Crane's Legs are Long

Seon (Korean: Seon, Japanese: Zen, Chinese: Chan) Master Baeg-Un ascended the hall and said, "It is completely provided in every person; it is perfected in every item, (so) how can you be amazed at me? Today I have nothing to do, so I will present you, my brethren, the proclamation of a turning word. Would you like that? Brethren, the crane's legs are long, the duck's legs are short, licorice is sweet, and pistachio is bitter. Do such words satisfy you?" He descended from the seat.

~ The Recorded Sayings of Baeg-Un (1299-1375) ~

Not to Die

A death-dealing blow to the I is at the same time a life-giving action. In Zen this is called the Great Death and the Great Renewal. To die the Great Death is to transcend life and death and achieve utter freedom. It makes the prospect of physical death secondary and unimportant. Zen Master Bunan put it this way:

Die while alive
And be thoroughly dead.
Then do what you will,
All is good.

When a master was told by a prospective student, "I would like to learn Zen from you," the master asked, "Are you prepared to die?"

The student replied, "I came here to learn Zen, not to die."

"If you can't die you will never learn Zen," responded the master.

~ The Zen of Living and Dying ~
~ Philip Kapleau ~

What do you need to practice Zen?

Great doubt!

Zen is built not on believing but on doubting. you must be prepared to take nothing for granted, to doubt everything.

The emperor summoned Daruma (Bodhidharma) and sought to impress him with a long list of good deeds he had done. In traditional Buddhist belief good deeds bring merit and a favourable rebirth.

"What is my merit?" concluded the sovereign.

"None at all," replied the sage in his grouchiest voice.

The emperor was not best pleased. "And who is he that addresses me?" he asked.

"No idea," answered Daruma, and left.

The doubt is one of the hardest concepts to get hold of. We are expected to know things, or at least pretend to know them. but without that great doubt you will never see Zen. if you want to understand the secrets of the koans, just raise the Don't Know Mind. You probably think that Don't know is passive. it isn't. Once you understand Don't Know you will have the secret of great power. It's not a power like the president has, more like the power of a great ocean. And it all starts with Don't Know.

~ Zen Questions ~
~ Robert Allen ~

Mushrooms

An intellectual went to a monastery to meet with an old monk who had a reputation as a wise man. He wished to discuss Buddha's nature with him, but the old man said, "I need to go to the kitchen to prepare some mushrooms."

The intellectual took offense. "But why? You are one of the greatest spirits in Zen and you want to prepare mushrooms? Leave those chores to your disciples."

The old man got up, and as he was leaving the room, he replied, "You have understood nothing about the path. I am going to prepare the mushrooms myself."

~ The Finger and the Moon: Zen Teachings and Koans ~
~ Alejandro Jodorowsky ~

Still Lacking

A monk on pilgrimage had visited great Masters without being able to settle what he felt still lacking. Rather dejected he came to Master Tokusan and asked him: 'Is it possible for me, too, to share the Supreme Teachings with the patriarchs?'

Master Tokusan hit him and said: 'What are you talking about?

Next day he asked for an explanation.

Master Tokusan said: 'My teaching has no words and sentences. It has nothing to give anybody.'

At this, the monk awakened.

~ The Wisdom of the Zen masters ~
~ Irmgard Schloegl ~

Meaning of Life

The student asked the Zen master:
"What is the meaning of life?"
The Zen master replied:
"Don't you have enough to worry about?"

~ When The Zen Dust Settles: Zen Koans Of A Retired
Zen Master ~
~ Rainer Loveiam ~

Tengu

The tengu, 'heavenly-dogs', are considered to be long-nosed goblins or demi-demons; they can also come in a form known as karasu-tengu that is half man and half crow.

One story of a tengu is as follows. Some boys were tormenting a bird and an old man passed by and saved the bird from dying. As he went on his way a mountain hermit came to him and thanked him, declaring that he was the bird he had saved. The traveller knew that instant that he was talking to a tengu. The tengu offered him supernatural powers in reward but the man said he had no need of them, and his only wish was to see the original Buddha giving a sermon. The tengu said he could transport him through time and space and show him such a thing, but that the man must say nothing and remain silent at all times. The man agreed, and the tengu took him to Vulture Mountain back in the time of the Buddha. There he saw hosts of spirits and demons and holy men listening to the Buddha. Unable to control himself, he cried out in reverence and that instant was transported back to his original position and to face a very angry tengu, who had his wings broken as punishment. The tengu scolded the man and was never seen again.

~ The Dark Side of Japan ~
~ Antony Cummins ~

Tengu and Kiuchi

Sometimes tengu steal people and return them in a demented state; this is referred to as tengu-kakushi or being 'hidden by a Tengu'. One example of this is Kiuchi, a samurai who went missing; his fellows came upon his equipment strewn around and, in the end, found him on a temple roof, at which point he told his story. He said that he had met with a black-robed monk and a larger man with a red face. They had told him that he must climb onto the temple roof, and when he refused, they broke his sword and scabbard and carried him to the roof. There they made him sit on a tray, and through magic they made the tray float; it took him through the skies to many regions across the land. After ten days of this, Kiuchi prayed to Buddha. The tray then landed on a mountain, but the mountain turned into the roof of the temple where he had begun.

~ The Dark Side of Japan ~
~ Antony Cummins ~

Jixing

JIXING entered a nunnery as a young girl, perhaps because her family was too poor to raise her. When she grew older, she visited a number of Buddhist masters and appears to have had an enlightenment experience as the result of her practice. She then took to wandering around begging for food. She made no effort to shelter herself from wind and rain, and bathed in the cold river. At first people took her for a madwoman and would not feed her. She gained a reputation for being able to forecast the future, however, and soon people found that blessings seemed to visit the household that invited her in as a guest. She also acquired a reputation for her wisdom and insight, expressed in simple and straightforward language.

Her poem:

I urge those of you who aspire to enlightenment —
In aspiring to enlightenment, you must be diligent!
If your mind is not completely sincere,
You will wallow forever in the bitter sea!
The great earth is vast and without limit,

And sentient beings are too many to count.
Yet how many people are there with the sense
To leap out of the bitterness of samsara?

~ Daughters Of Emptiness ~
~ Beata Grant ~

One

A monk drew four strokes in front of Master Baso, with the top stroke being long and the lower three being short. he said, "Without saying that one stroke is long and three are short; leaving all words; cutting out all arguments - please, master, answer."

Baso then drew one stroke, saying, "Without saying one stroke is long and three are short, I have answered you."

~ Case 56 of Master Kido's 100 Koans ~

Not Hard

Master Anzan went into the mill to see Master Sekishitsu. He said, "It is not easy, is it?"

Sekishitsu said, "What is so hard about it? You fetch it in a bottomless bowl and take it away in a formless tray."

Anzan was speechless.

~ Case 22 of Master Kido's 100 Koans ~

Kakuzan Shido's Dagger

JAPAN, THIRTEENTH CENTURY

THE NUN Kakuzan Shido trained at the notoriously tough Rinzai monastery Engakuji. Her teacher, Tokei (whose name meant "Peach Tree Valley"), gave her inka, transmission and authority to be an independent teacher.

In the transmission ceremony, Shido took the seat in front of the altar and the monks asked her questions to test her skill. When it was the head monk's turn, he challenged her: "In our lineage, anyone who receives inka must give a discourse on the sutras. Are you really capable of doing this?"

Shido pulled out the ten-inch dagger carried by all women of the warrior class and held it in front of his face. "Every Zen teacher in the lineage of our master should teach the sutras," she said. "But I am a woman of the warrior line and I speak the Dharma face to face, with my dagger drawn. What need do I have for books?" He persisted with another question. "What was your original understanding before your parents were born?"

She answered by sitting in silence with her eyes closed. Then she said, "Do you understand?"

The head monk answered with a verse:
Here in Peach Tree Valley,
a wine gourd has been drained to the last drop.
Drunken eyes see ten miles of flowers.
Shido replied, "Was I not directed to the Way even before
the births of my mother and father?"

~ The Hidden Lamp: Stories from Twenty-Five Centuries
of Awakened Women ~
~ Zoketsu Norman Fischer ~

Tranquility

Someone asked, "Master, could you please teach me the state of true tranquillity?"

Joshu's answer: "If I teach you, it won't be tranquil anymore."

~ Case 351 of Radical Zen ~

Plato

A student, struggling with the abstract concepts of Platonic mathematics, asked Plato, "What practical end do these theorems serve? What is to be gained from them?"

Plato turned to his attendant slave and said, "Give this young man an obol [a small coin] that he may feel that he has gained something from my teachings, and then expel him."

The White Stone

A master is holding a bowl in his hands at the moment a disciple asks him this enigmatic question: "Master, how do we break the white stone in a pile of garbage?"

The master lets the bowl fall to the floor, and as it breaks in a thousand pieces he responds, "Like this."

~ The Finger and the Moon: Zen Teachings and Koans ~
~ Alejandro Jodorowsky ~

Can I turn back?

Looking for Zen is not like looking for a lost coin. Once you start to look for Zen, it starts looking for you. People sometimes ask if it is possible to give up and go back to the life they lived before. The short answer is "No." I gave up on Zen twice, or thought I had. Each time, eventually, something drew me back to it. Nor had I gone "rusty" as you do when you leave other skills unused. It was very clear that, even though I had been unaware of it, my Zen had continued to develop in spite of my apparent indifference. I know others who have had the same experience. In fact, there are some well-documented cases in which the act of giving up was the very thing that precipitated the experience of satori.

There is a story of a monk who, after many years of trying, decided that he was never going to experience satori. He thought he might just as well make himself useful around the monastery, cleaning, cooking, and generally looking after the more talented monks. As soon as he made that decision enlightenment struck.

~ Zen Questions ~

~ Robert Allen ~

Why Cry?

When Zen master Tung-shan felt it was time for him to go, he had his head shaved, took a bath, put on his robe, rang the bell to bid farewell to the community, and sat up till he breathed no more. To all appearances he had died. Thereupon the whole community burst out crying grievously as little children do at the death of their mother. Suddenly the master opened his eyes and said to the weeping monks, "We monks are supposed to be detached from all things transitory. In this consists true spiritual life. To live is to work, to dies is to rest. What is the use of groaning and moaning?" He then ordered a "stupidity-purifying" meal for the whole community. After the meal he said to them, "Please make no fuss over me! Be calm as befits a family of monks! Generally speaking, when anyone is at the point of going, he was no use for noise and commotion." Thereupon he returned to the Abbot's room, where he sat up as in meditation till he passed away.

~ The Zen of Living and Dying ~
~ Philip Kapleau ~

Vowing not to spread out the coverlet

Zen teacher Shouxun of Buddha Lamp Temple was a disciple of Fojian. He went to follow the congregation into the hall to ask for instruction, but it was crowded and there was no room for him. He lamented, "If I do not get total realization in this life, I swear never to spread out my coverlet to sleep."

From then on, he stood there leaning against a pillar for forty-nine days, as if mourning for his dead mother, until he attained great enlightenment.

Nature Painting

The Sung masters were pre-eminently landscape painters, creators of a tradition of "nature painting" which has hardly been surpassed anywhere in the world. For it shows us the life of nature–of mountains, waters, mists, rocks, trees, and birds–as felt by Taoism and Zen. It is a world to which man belongs but which he does not dominate; it is sufficient to itself, for it was not "made for" anyone and has no purpose of its own. As Hsuan-chueh said:

Over the river, the shining moon; in the pine trees, sighing wind;

All night long so tranquil–why? And for whom?

~ The Way of Zen: Alan Watts ~

Undistracted

Utame was only fifteen years old when she first received instruction from an enlightened Zen nun, who taught her how to look into the innermost self.

Utame plunged into meditation day and night, paying no attention to anything else. Even when she was at her mirror putting on makeup, she was inwardly looking into the essence of mind. Sometimes she would become so absorbed that she would forget what she was doing and just sit there silently.

Now her parents, who had no idea what lay behind their daughter's strange behavior, began to think she might be suffering from depression or heading for a nervous breakdown. They tried to get her to go out to the theater and take trips to scenic places, but Utame had no desire for any of these diversions.

Finally one day her efforts came to fruition, and the young woman's mind opened up in great enlightenment.

Later Utame married and bore four children, two sons and two daughters. Her husband had the misfortune to go bankrupt, so Utame took up needlework to help support the family. She lived to be more than seventy years old, eventually passing away one day in a state of serene repose.

~ Zen Antics ~

~ Thomas Cleary ~

Yikui

YIKUI (1625–79) was one of the seven Dharma heirs of Master Xinggang. The great-granddaughter of a Minister of Justice and the daughter of a scholar-painter, Yikui had two sisters and two brothers, one of whom, Zilin, would play a particularly central role in her life. Yikui was by all accounts a precociously intelligent girl, who not only mastered the feminine arts of sewing and embroidery, but also excelled in the arts of painting and poetry writing. She married a young scholar and apparently fulfilled all of the requirements of a good wife and daughter-in-law happily and successfully. In the fall of 1648, however, her husband, with whom she had a companionate marriage, passed away, leaving Yikui a widow at the age of twenty-three.

After her husband's death, Yikui retreated to her room, where she remained in seclusion, eating a minimal vegetarian diet and engaging in single-minded Buddha-recitation (nianfo). Later, she became interested in Chan meditation and sought out the guidance of Master Xinggang, under whom she eventually took ordination. Yikui lived for a few years at the Crouching Lion Convent, but after Master Xinggang's death, moved into a lovely hermitage located on the riverbank, which had been built for her by her brother Zilin and which was named Cantong Cloister, or "Cloister of Investigating Commonality." The cloister quickly developed into a fairly large establishment, and Master Yikui attracted a great number of disciples.

This seemingly idyllic life came to an abrupt end in 1667 when, seven years after taking over the leadership of the Crouching Lion Convent, Master Xing-gang's designated successor and Yikui's Dharma sister, Yigong, fell ill from exhaustion and overwork. Not long after, the forty-six-year-old Yigong passed away, but not before formally designating Yikui as her successor. After six tiring but productive years as abbess of the Crouching Lion, Yikui moved back to her beloved hermitage, where she died in 1679 at the age of fifty-four. Her own collection of religious discourses and other writings was compiled several years before her death.

Unable to Sleep Because of a Cold

My whole body burns with fever, I cannot keep from coughing,

Rising, I sit, my robes pulled about me; my breath slowly clears.

As I emerge from a state of samadhi the hourglass has run out;

All I hear is the sound of neighbors' dogs barking in the town.

~ Daughters of Emptiness ~
~ Beata Grant ~

Bird Daughters

There was once a man called Okada who was a ronin who loved to hunt. Often, he would go into the wild with muskets loaded to shoot birds. His two daughters hated this sport and pleaded with him to stop, but he continued his bloodthirsty hobby. So, one moonlit evening, they dressed as two white storks and went to his hunting ground. From afar he thought them birds and took aim, shooting and killing both. Upon inspection, to his horror he discovered that he had killed his own children. After this he shaved his head and became a monk and never killed again.

~ The Dark Side of Japan ~
~ Antony Cummins ~

Zen Master Yamamoto

At the time of his death, he was the abbot of a large and respected monastery in Japan. Having grown old - he was ninety-six at the time, if I remember correctly - he was almost completely deaf and blind. No longer able to actively teach his students, he made an announcement that it was time for him to take his leave, and that he would die at the start of the new year. He then stopped eating. The monks in his temple reminded him that the New Year period was the busiest time at the temple, and that for him to die then would be most inconvenient. "I see," he said, and he resumed eating until the early summer, when he again stopped eating and then one day toppled over and quietly slipped away.

~ The Zen of Living and Dying ~
~ Philip Kapleau ~

Forgetting sleep and food

Zen Master Yue of Songyuan [1132-1202] studied first as a layman with Hua of Ying-an, but he did not reach accord with him.

He spurred himself on even more, and went to see Jie of Mi-an, who answered whatever he asked. Mi-an sighed and said, "This is only cut and dried Zen."

Yue's efforts became even more intense, to the point that he forgot to sleep or eat. It so happened that Mi-an was in his private room questioning a monk [about the koan], "It is not mind, it is not Buddha, it is not things: what is it?"

Yue, who was standing by his side, was greatly enlightened.

The house with the golden windows

The little girl lived in a small, very simple, poor house on a hill and as she grew she would play in the small garden and as she grew she was able to see over the garden fence and across the valley to a wonderful house high on the hill - and this house had golden windows, so golden and shining that the little girl would dream of how magic it would be to grow up and live in a house with golden windows instead of an ordinary house like hers.

And although she loved her parents and her family, she yearned to live in such a golden house and dreamed all day about how wonderful and exciting it must feel to live there.

When she got to an age where she gained enough skill and sensibility to go outside her garden fence, she asked her mother is she could go for a bike ride outside the gate and down the lane. After pleading with her, her mother finally allowed her to go, insisting that she kept close to the house and didn't wander too far. The day was beautiful, and the little girl knew exactly where she was heading! Down the lane and across the valley, she rode her bike until she got to the gate of the golden house across on the other hill.

As she dismounted her bike and lent it against the gate post, she focused on the path that lead to the house and then on the house itself...and was so disappointed as she realised all the windows were plain and rather dirty, reflecting nothing other than the sad neglect of the house that stood derelict.

So sad she didn't go any further and turned, heartbroken as she remounted her bike ... As she glanced up, she saw a sight to amaze her...there across the way on her side of the valley was a little house and its windows glistened golden ...as the sun shone on her little home.

She realised that she had been living in her golden house and all the love and care she found there was what made her home the 'golden house'. Everything she dreamed was right there in front of her nose!

What ways are there?

Master Kuzan came to see Master Seppo. The moment he entered the gate, Seppo grabbed him and said, "What is it?"

Kuzan was enlightened. He raised his hands, waving them about.

Seppo said, "In what way did you come to understand?"

Kuzan said, "What ways are there?'

Seppo acknowledged Kuzan's enlightenment.

~ Case 26 of Master Kido's 100 Koans ~

Hui-neng's Departure

On the eighth of July, Zen master Hui-neng (638-713), the sixth Chinese patriarch of Zen, announced to his monks, "Gather around me. I have decided to leave this world in the eighth month."

When the monks heard this, many of them wept openly.

"For whom are you crying?" the master asked. "Are you worrying about me because you think I don't know where I'm going? If I didn't know, I wouldn't be able to leave you this way. What you are really crying about is that you don't know where I'm going. If you actually knew, you couldn't possibly cry, because True-nature is without birth or death, without going or coming..."

~ The Zen of Living and Dying ~
~ Philip Kapleau ~

Nothing Spoken

"Subhūti, what do you think? Is there any Dharma spoken by the Tathāgata?"
Subhūti said to the Buddha. "No, World Honored One, nothing has been spoken by the Tathāgata." ||Ch. 13 ||

Buddha said to Subhūti, "Subhūti, do not say the Tathāgata has the thought, 'I have spoken dharma.' Do not think that way. And why? If someone says the Tathāgata has spoken dharma, he slanders the Buddha due to his inability to understand what I say." ||Ch. 21||

~ The Diamond Sutra, Chapter 13, 21 ~

Nothing Attained

Subhūti said to the Buddha, "World Honored One, is it that the Tathāgata in attaining Anuttarasamyaksambodhi (Unparalleled Perfect Enlightenment) did not attain anything?"

The Buddha said, "So it is, so it is, Subhūti. As to Anuttarasamyaksambodhi, there is not even the slightest dharma which I could attain, therefore it is called Anuttarasamyaksambodhi."

~ The Diamond Sutra, Chapter 22 ~

True Virtue

When Yang Tzu went to the Sung State, he passed a night at an inn. The innkeeper had: two concubines--one beautiful, the other ugly. The latter he loved; the former he hated. Yang Tzu asked how this was; whereupon one of the inn servants said: "The beautiful one is so conscious of her beauty that one does not think her beautiful. The ugly one is so conscious of her ugliness that one does not think her ugly."

"Note this, my disciples!" cried Yang.

"Be virtuous, but without being consciously so; and wherever you go, you will be beloved."

~ Zhuangzi ~
[This story is also there in the Book of Lieh Tzu.]

Illogical Announcement

A Zen master produces his staff before his congregation and declares: "You do not call it a staff. What would you call it?" Someone comes out of the audience, takes the master's staff away from him, breaks it into two, and throws it down. All this is the outcome of the master's illogical announcement.

Another master, holding up his staff, says: "If you have one, I give you mine; if you have none, I will take it away from you." There is no rationalism in this.

Still another master once gave this sermon: "When you know what this staff is, you know all, you have finished the study of Zen." Without further remark he left the hall.

~ Zen and Japanese Culture ~
~ D.T. Suzuki ~

Zen

There is a story of a Zen monk who, after many years of trying, could not find enlightenment. He went to his abbot and asked for permission to withdraw, which was granted. Having left the monastery, where he had lived in strict celibacy, he felt the need of a woman. He went to the red-light district and found himself a prostitute. Just as they started to have sex, enlightenment struck.

~ Zen Questions ~
~ Robert Allen ~

Keep Meditating Continuously

Zen Master Taixu, once said, "If you have not yet completely awakened, you must go to the meditation cushion and sit impassively for ten, twenty, thirty years, observing your original face before your father and mother were born."

Bonus: A Story

Once upon a time, there was a mountain, and on the mountain, there was a temple, and in the temple, there was an old monk and a little monk. One day, the old monk said to the little monk: 'I tell you a story. Once upon a time, there was a mountain, and on the mountain, there was a temple, and in the temple there's an old monk and a little monk. One day, the old monk said to the little monk: 'I tell you a story...'

Bibliography

1. The Zen Teaching of Bodhidharma, Translated by Red Pine
2. The Record of Rinzai
3. Zen's Chinese Heritage by Andy Ferguson
4. Records of the Transmission of the Lamp (Jingde Chuandeng Lu, Vol 1-6) by Daoyuan, translated by Randolph S. Whitfield
5. Treasury of the Forest of Ancestors by Satyavayu
6. Zen Flesh, Zen Bones by Nyogen Senzaki and Paul Reps
7. Radical Zen (Recorded Sayings of Joshu) by Yoel Hoffman
8. The Recorded Sayings of Zen Master Joshu, Translated by James Green
9. Talking about Food Doesn't Appease Hunger: Phrases on hunger in Chan (Zen) Buddhist texts by Anu Niemi
10. Hekiganroku (The Blue Cliff Record)
11. Shoyoroku
12. Mumonkan

13. Mumonkan (Originally titled 'Zen and Zen Classics, Vol. 4'), Translated by R.H. Blyth
14. Dogen's 300 Koans
15. Shobogenzo by Dogen
16. Zen Koans by Venerable Gyomay M. Kubose
17. Zen Speaks: Shouts of Nothingness by Tsai Chih Chung
18. The Original Teachings of Ch'an Buddhism by Chang Ching Yuan
19. The Golden Age of Zen: Zen Masters of the T'ang by John Ching Hsiung Wu
20. Zen, The Path of Paradox, Vol 3 by Osho
21. A Bird on the Wing by Osho
22. Entangling Vines: A Classic Collection of Zen Koans by Thomas Yuho Kirchner
23. Sun-Face Buddha: The Teachings of Ma-tsu and the Hung-chou School of Ch'an; Introduced and Translated by Cheng Chien Bhikshu
24. The Records of Mazu and the Making of Classical Chan Literature by Mario Poceski
25. (Collected Works of Korean Buddhism, Volume 3) Hyujeong, Selected Works Edited and Translated by John Jorgensen
26. (Collected Works of Korean Buddhism, Volume 7-1) Gongan Collections I Edited and Translated by John Jorgensen
27. (Collected Works of Korean Buddhism, Volume 7-2) Gongan Collections II Edited and Translated by John Jorgensen

28. (Collected Works of Korean Buddhism, Volume 8) Seon Dialogues, Edited and Translated by John Jorgensen

29. Being Peace by Thich Nhat Hahn

30. One Bird One Stone: 108 American Zen Stories by Sean Murphy

31. Records of Yunmen (Master Yunmen, From the Record of the Chan Teacher "Gate of the Clouds" published by Kodansha International)

32. The Warrior Koans

33. The Old Zen Master, Translated by Trevor Leggett

34. Take It Easy, Vol 1, by Osho

35. Dang Dang Doko Dang by Osho

36. The Path of Love by Osho

37. The Buddha, The Emptiness Of The Heart by Osho

38. Zen: The Mystery and The Poetry of The Beyond by Osho

39. A Sudden Clash of Thunder by Osho

40. Meditating with Koans by Zhuhong, Translated by J. C. Cleary

41. The Zen Reader by Thomas Cleary

42. Ecstasy, The Forgotten Language by Osho

43. Kyozan, A True Man of Zen by Osho

44. Zen: The Quantum Leap from Mind to No Mind by Osho

45. Zen Masters of China by Richard Bryan McDaniel

46. Zen Masters of Japan by Richard Bryan McDaniel

47. Japanese Death Poems by Yoel Hoffman

48. The Iron Flute: 100 Zen Koans by Nyogen Senzaki, Ruth Strout-McCandless

49. The Zen Doctrine of No-Mind by D. T. Suzuki

50. Zen and Zen Classics, Vol 3, by R.H. Blyth

51. Every End Exposed: The 100 Koans of Master Kido - With the Answers of Hakuin – Zen

52. Alagaddupama Sutta

53. The Lotus Sutra

54. Record of the life of the Ch'an master Po-chang Huai-hai [Bojang Whyhigh] Translated by Gary Snyder

55. Ordinary Mind as the Way: The Hongzhou School and the Growth of Chan Buddhism By Mario Poceski

56. The Zen Teaching of Huang Po on the Transmission of Mind, Translated by John Blofeld

57. Zen Mind, Beginner's Mind by Shunryu Suzuki

58. Bring me the Rhinoceros by John Tarrant

59. Teaching Letters of Zen Master Seung Sahn

60. Zen Antics by Thomas Cleary

61. Web Resources:

    1. http://www.sinc.sunysb.edu/Clubs/buddhism/story/story.html

    2. Zen Humor: Classic Humor from the Zen - Chan - Son Buddhist Tradition by Timothy Conway https://www.enlightened-spirituality.org/Zen_Humor.html

    3. http://poetrychina.net/Story_of_Zen/zenstory13.htm